Training Triage

Performance-Based Solutions Amid Chaos, Confusion, and Change

Includes CD-ROM

 ASTD Press

Lou Russell

ASTD Press is an internationally renowned source of insightful and practical information on workplace learning and performance topics, including training basics, evaluation and return-on-investment (ROI), instructional systems development (ISD), e-learning, leadership, and career development.

Ordering information: Books published by ASTD Press can be purchased by visiting our Website at store.astd.org or by calling 800.628.2783 or 703.683.8100.

Library of Congress Control Number: 2005933865

ISBN: 1-56286-409-2

Acquisitions and Development Editor: Mark Morrow
Copyeditor: Karen Eddleman
Interior Design and Production: Kathleen Schaner
Cover Design: Renita Wade
Cover Illustration: Nigel Sandor

Printed by Victor Graphics, Inc., Baltimore, Maryland, www.victorgraphics.com.

Contents

Preface

Once upon a time, there were three brave and beautiful business people, Prince Will, Princess Beam, and King Roy. Each of these brave and beautiful people tossed and turned night after night because their business was just not right.

Prince Will was sad. He was very good at what he did at work and always stepped forward to volunteer to learn new things. His bosses counted on him to do the impossible, and he always delivered. Each time, though, he feared he might let someone down. One fateful day, he was given a new software package to use and a new process to go with it but he couldn't figure it out from the manuals, which seemed to be written in a strange, foreign language. He was afraid that Prince Will soon would be Prince Won't.

Prince Will Googled "big learning" and found a slick, animated Website by a company called Big Learning Results. Mere moments after he called, three tall men in navy blue suits appeared in his lobby. They knew exactly how to fix Prince Will's problem. Prince Will sighed with relief. As he watched them walk away, leaving behind strong handshakes and 5-page full-color brochures, he knew the answer was just days away.

The next day Prince Will received a beautifully printed proposal via overnight delivery. To his dismay, the Big Learning Results company proposed to spend 6 months studying Prince Will's problem and then creating a custom e-learning experience for him that they could deliver in 1 year. Prince Will nearly passed out when he saw that the 1-year solution would cost him $50,000! Prince Will was sadder than ever.

Princess Beam had a different sort of problem. She was the project manager of a very important strategic project. She supervised a team responsible for installing WIFI Internet access for the entire castle. The technology was challenging but not impossible because they had plenty of funding, experts who knew what they were doing, and sponsorship that was strong. What could go wrong? Princess Beam, however, tossed and turned at night because she knew in her good heart that her team members were individual stars who disliked each other tremendously. So far, this had all rumbled under the surface, but there were some big milestones approaching and Princess Beam knew that the project was slipping because people were avoiding each other.

She called a friend of hers from another kingdom and asked if her friend had ever had this problem. Her friend said that she once knew someone that solved this problem by making everyone attend a 1-day workshop taught by a famous company called Leadership in Under 8 Hours. This solution seemed ideal! Princess Beam called and scheduled the class immediately.

The team wasn't too sure about the workshop and attended begrudgingly. Some team members were late and some left early. Each of them learned the five types of teams, the 13 rules of meetings, the 42 leadership competencies, and the . . . well, you get the picture. The snacks were good, the chairs too hard, and very little changed with the team. Princess Beam was now Princess Beat.

King Roy had much bigger problems. He was in charge of the largest kingdom in the country. The country used to make money from the citizens who could weave straw into gold. Recently, a synthetic gold had been invented across the sea. The synthetic gold was stronger, cheaper, and looked better on your finger. This development was seriously cutting into the economy, and, for the first time ever, people did not have enough work or money. King Roy needed to do something to return the country to prosperity.

King Roy issued a request for proposals, and three companies responded. The Big Results Company suggested that they study this problem for 12 months before determining the problem for $150,000. The Leadership in Under 8 Hours company proposed a 3-day workshop to fix these types of problems for $10,000 plus travel. A new company called It's Your Fault Consulting proposed that they would coach King Roy each day for an hour for $350 per session. This would help him more completely solve every problem that came up. King Roy thought that all the solutions were expensive, vague, and inadequate, for he was a very wise king.

You rarely hear what happens when queens retire, but several queens in the kingdom had retired from their jobs and were quite bored. In their previous careers, they had sold castles, written castle software, and even worked at the castle bank so they knew a great deal about castles. Bored with retirement, they named themselves the Training Triage Fairies and set about trying to help people solve their own problems.

They didn't want to be a company like the Big Results Company because they didn't want to study a problem forever. They didn't want to be like Leadership in Under 8 Hours because they knew that workshops aren't always enough help. It's Your Fault Consulting just seemed like bad karma.

The Training Triage Fairies thought it might be fun to figure out a way to take the best of each company's approach and try to help people. They believed if they offered reasonable prices that they might have some fun helping other people, supporting their families, and buying chocolate, which they kept in constant supply. They really liked to have fun and thought that other people might like to have fun, too, on their way to improving things. After all, everyone is different and every problem is different, but fun is always constant.

The Training Triage Fairies met Prince Will at a coffee shop on 96th Street and listened to his sad story. They realized that Prince Will just had a skills and knowledge problem and needed a little training to jumpstart his work. They set up some training for him on his new software and processes and after a week, Prince Won't was back to Prince Will.

One of the Training Triage Fairies was speaking at the Castle WIFI World Conference and met Princess Beam. Princess Beam started asking WIFI questions, but it was soon apparent that her team was the issue. The Queens worked with the team to figure out their individual strengths and weaknesses using a series of straightforward assessments. The Fairies helped the team set up some ground rules, and the project was a WIFI success. Guess what Princess Beam was doing—beaming!

Sadly, the Training Triage Fairies were on a cruise when King Roy sent out his request for proposals. When they returned, they were surprised to find out that the problem had not been solved by It's Your Fault's coaching approach. The Fairies talked with King Roy, and suddenly he realized that they could make wheat into food!

This would be a very complicated undertaking because the workers were so used to making gold. The Training Triage Fairies helped King Roy build a plan and hold people accountable. This approach required new job descriptions, incentives, new processes, and even new facilities, but after a year, the improvement was obvious. In fact, King Roy won the King Entrepreneur of the Year for his innovative approach to the problem.

The Training Triage Fairies have a much bigger story to tell than most people realize. They hope you will share this book with others who would benefit from focusing on the right solution for the right problem. You, too, can apply the Training Triage approach to achieve results while having fun!

Thanks to the training fairies at RMA—Vija, Margie, and Carol—and the princesses at home—Kelly, Kristin, and Katherine—for all they do. Of course, I must also acknowledge my knight in shining armor, Doug Martin. This book is dedicated to training fairy Susan Vaughn who has lived a chaotic fairytale with us. Her abilities astound us, and her students are better off having known her.

And they all lived happily ever after.

Lou Russell
October 2005

chapter 1

Introduction

Why Training Feels Like Emergency Room Triage

Evolution of This Book

In 1981, while I was working as a young programmer at AT&T, my boss approached me with a funny look on his face. "I need to talk to you," he said as we moved into a conference room. "Would you consider becoming a trainer?" His face revealed his embarrassment for having to ask me to take such a horrible job. "Yes!" I exclaimed, thus beginning a wonderful adventure. Turns out, this "training thing" was my calling.

I was shipped off for training at AT&T headquarters in New Jersey. I was going to be teaching system development and project management methodologies, which were brand new to us at Indiana Bell. I attended two 5-day workshops: train-the-trainer and advanced train-the-trainer. To become certified in a class, I had to attend it twice. Highly detailed instructor notes gave detailed descriptions of almost every factor one might encounter in a training session down to how many ashtrays should be in the room. (Okay, now I'm dating myself!)

Bell Labs had done a great deal of research on how people learn and how we should teach so that learning was maximized. One weird study had shown that students don't like corners in training rooms because they make them feel nervous. So, the training rooms had no corners, just rounded walls. The walls were painted in three color bands that drew the eye to the trainer level.

When I returned from my training immersion, I created a schedule of courses, most of which were 5 days in length. Back in the days of the telecommunications monopoly, we could attend almost unlimited training, a benefit that I appreciate to this day. We had coffee and donuts in all classes. Every 6 months or so, we'd publish a new schedule and people would sign up for the offerings. Soon we had added video libraries and additional classes, and our data-processing department's training grew into what might be called today a corporate university.

Some of you may have worked in the training field at this time. Many of you may think I made this story up. Contrast this overflowing-cup environment to what happened only 2 years later.

First, AT&T broke into pieces and deregulation began. Early retirements were offered, and I took one to start my training company. My peers in corporate training, who were now my customers, were being forced to do more with less. Many were laid off in business tsunamis that continue even now. There were mergers and acquisitions and dot-bombs and terrorists, and training was usually the first item to go.

In case you weren't there, let me explain how this book fits into the story. First, the company's training catalogs disappeared, replaced with large video libraries. Then the video libraries disappeared, and so did training itself for awhile. Companies still depended on training events if there was a problem but only when the budget hadn't been cut yet. There was no accountability, and the common strategy of sitting through 2 days of something was supposed to "fix" people. Training that emphasized process improvement gave way to training that taught technology. Thanks to the fears of Y2K, good, old technical training was dusted off and revitalized, and I'm not ashamed to say many of us had a couple of really good years. However, most of those information technology training companies are gone now.

Then, something great began to happen. Many people in different places and using different words began to say out loud that workshops didn't work, no matter what media was being used. Eventually, the term "performance consulting" emerged, but is still a code word only used among us training people. The philosophy was changing. To really affect people's performance required more than just a workshop. Strategies to improve performance might include a variety of interventions, but, to be successful, they had to include a clear understanding of the business challenge, involve aligned job descriptions and performance reviews, have strong sponsorship, and entail measurements to prove that progress was being made. Trainers were becoming consultants, which some thought meant we were all going to the dark side.

Meanwhile, back in the business world, things were getting crazy. A recession hit in 2001. Terrorists struck on September 11. Staff was cut dramatically to save companies. Trainers were out. Any training that was done was outsourced. The company had to be absolutely desperate to fund anything and so demanded complete customization from training firms. Because the world was now operating at Web-speed, the customized, emergency training/performance consulting had to be delivered yesterday. Engineers, computer technologists, project managers, and training people started talking among themselves about developing solutions faster, cheaper, and with higher quality. Anyone trying to sell a 6-month needs analysis was not-so-subtly shown the door.

So, you have training moving to performance consulting, adopting a strategy that was bigger, faster, and more complex, not to mention company-saving. Except for a period of overemphasis on e-learning ("It can all be fixed with Web-based training"), the old concept of a trainer had matured into an important player getting closer to the boardroom. Not all companies were forward thinking, but the trend was in place.

Flash forward: In 2004, ASTD published a competency study titled *Mapping the Future*. In this research document, ASTD continues to work toward expanding our field from the single focus on training to the more systemic focus, beyond just human and organization development to workplace learning and performance.

The Rescue Squad

This year, when the phones ring in our offices, people are not asking for the 2-day generic project management class like they would have just 2 or 3 years ago. Thank goodness, they no longer ask for a 1-day leadership class, which, in my humble opinion, is as useful as the old video libraries. Today they call and ask for help. Here are some of the calls we get:

- "Help! The members of my critical project team hate each other!"

- "Help! Our company is growing aggressively, but to hit our goals will require all our managers to mature into more effective leaders and especially coaches."

- "Help! Our policies and procedures are not tight, and compliance is a huge priority for our board (and the U.S. Department of Justice)!"

- "Help! We are going through a huge change and need to transform *now*."

- "Help! We need to get our folks to improve their customer service, but they also really need to buy into the customer service philosophy; that's the only way our company can survive."

And, all too often, I hear "Can you be here in a week? In a day? This afternoon?" Trainers all over are getting the same calls.

This book is not for the baby trainer, the newbie who has been given the task to manage the e-learning library, or teach a 1-day benefits class, or find a vendor to teach a project management workshop. This book is designed for people with some scars from the wars that have passed, people who are trusted at their companies because they care about the learners and the business and will do what it takes to help. This book assumes that you have the lingo down (whether Mager or Bloom or Kirkpatrick), have a good-enough classroom technique, have informal networks with

> The eight recent trends driving this evolution are defined by the ASTD research as:
>
> 1. Drastic times, drastic measures—the impact of uncertain economic conditions
>
> 2. Blurred lines: life or work?—new technology and ways to work
>
> 3. Small world and shrinking—global interdependency
>
> 4. New faces, new expectations—the diverse workforce
>
> 5. Work be nimble, work be quick—increased pressure to work quickly
>
> 6. Security alert!—safety and security concerns
>
> 7. Life and work in the e-lane—Internet-driven societies
>
> 8. A higher ethical bar—ethics and integrity.

executives and leaders to get things done, and have struggled with return-on-investment (ROI) evaluation.

So, you are getting calls asking for the impossible to be delivered the next day, too. As if that weren't enough of a challenge, you have very little staff anymore, and even less budget. And you *know* that this business problem has to be tackled, and as Jerry Garcia said roughly, ". . . it's terribly pathetic that it has to be you." You matter, and you can help.

The Triage Approach

This book is broken into problem phone calls. I have taken my most frequent requests; shared with you the business problem and constraints; listed the quick, requirement-gathering questions that I asked; and then described the facilitation, simulation, and training techniques that I whipped together. I've included many activities, tools, and instruments that you can adapt to your own practice. Each chapter has ideas about how to measure the improvement although, as you know, this is a bit more complex than it seems and is often outside the scope of what a trainer can do on his or her own.

Each chapter is built on a template, and icons flag some of the main points:

 What They Say—The Situation: a scripted problem

 What You Hear: questioning and listening between the words

 What You Do: a whole solution

 Your Triage Intervention: overview

 What You Build: step-by-step details

 Top Priority: the absolute requirements for successful implementation of the triage intervention.

Most of the techniques are unique, but there is a little overlap. You'll see my prejudice toward a couple of things that I like to start with. I am a huge believer in assessments. In the chapters, you'll read that I often rely on DISC. DISC is a Jungian-based behavioral assessment that is offered by multiple vendors. Over the years, different vendors have assigned different meanings to the letters in the DISC acronym, although the developer William Marston (also the inventor of the lie detector) defined the DISC model as Dominance; Influence or Inducement; Steadiness or Stability; and Compliance, Conscientiousness, or Caution.

Another of my favorite assessments is called PIAV (personal interests, attitudes, and values). If there is an assessment that your company uses, simply substitute it. If you'd like more information about these two, please email me. I like to use surveys to start these sessions as well, including 360-degree assessments.

I have tried to give you enough background so that you understand why I chose what I did. Each intervention starts with learning objectives, which I think are critical to project management and measurement. I suspect it would be rare that you would be able to just plop my chapter into your world, so please, pick and choose and build the solution that fits the company you know best: yours.

How to Use This Book

I did not design this book to be read cover to cover. Instead, I hope you will browse through the chapters and find the situations that are the most like the ones you have been getting calls about. Most of the techniques are unique, but there is some overlap in a few chapters. This is really not a training technique book. You will find detailed guidelines that are designed to help guide you through training situations. I'm counting on your experience to give you the adaptability you will need to use these ideas for your problems.

 Also, throughout the chapters you'll encounter a CD icon. This indicates that the particular activity or tool can be found on the companion CD, both in PDF format as well as in Microsoft Word.

Here's the general flow of how I react to these phone calls and how these chapters are arranged:

- *Analysis of requirements (listen, ask, collect data):* Asking great questions is critical to success with performance consulting. Learn to ask and listen. Ask questions from many different directions. Be a detective or an anthropologist at your company. Look for answers in untraditional places, like over a casual cup of coffee at the coffee bar.

- *Prerequisite assessment:* This step includes collecting data to prove the issue exists, data to clarify the issue, data (personal assessments) to make it pertinent to you, and a baseline to measure from. Surveys and assessments are great prework for all these reasons. These instruments give you data for the session that came from the learners themselves or from their customers, for example. It's very hard to argue with a rationale built in this way.

- *Simulation:* Try to re-create the problem in class, but in a safe, metaphorical way. Set up simulations to help people catch each other in the very dynamics you are trying to improve. Always debrief as long as the simulation itself, and prepare these questions carefully. The learning happens during the debriefing.

- *Facilitation:* Use positive, problem-solving, process-flow techniques that are efficacious in a training environment. A performance consultant is a facilitator of learning, not a trainer. Many of these techniques are facilitation techniques rather than training techniques.

- *Action plans:* Never let them leave without closing the deal just like a salesperson. Get a commitment from them as a team or individual. Ask them to put some skin in the game.

- *Follow-up strategy:* Always do a review after each project. Find out how the owner of the problem views the progress. Be prepared to continue the journey with different techniques, encouraging the participants to look at the problem from a new perspective.

- *Post-assessment or measurement:* Formally measure the results of the time together and the impact on the business problem. This will probably require some new assessment questions different from the ones you use after training.

There are a couple of other things you should know about me. I am a passionate supporter of experiential learning. I believe people learn best by self-discovery, especially when complex problems are involved. These interventions are not for teaching Microsoft Word, although I think self-discovery works pretty well with that, too. Complex business problems require addressing some skills and knowledge gaps but, more important, they require addressing the motivations of the learners. That's not a place where lecture works. Remember my motto: "Lecture is a last resort."

I have kept an eye on Howard Gardner's theory of multiple intelligences as I developed these interventions. By design, the techniques balance the different needs of different learners. For example, I fluctuate between intrapersonal techniques (alone) and interpersonal techniques (team). It is important that people be able to learn and grow in an environment that is easy for them. If you don't know about multiple intelligences research and how it affects learning, you can read more about it in my first book, *The Accelerated Learning Fieldbook* (1999, Jossey-Bass).

Who Me, a Project Manager?

I am passionate about project management. I am not a detail person by nature, so I have had to create project management discipline for myself. Here are a few project management beliefs I have:

- Shortages of time, money, subject matter experts (SMEs), support, and so forth will always be factors. A good project manager cheerfully works within these often fluctuating constraints. Whining about how unfair they seem is a waste of the few resources you have.

- Don't have too many meetings and don't have too many people at the meetings.

- It may seem like the opposite, but you can't communicate too much. Face-to-face, one-on-one is best. Email is the worst.

- Do a good job asking questions at the beginning, even hard questions. Nothing else helps as much as that.

- Never get mad at the SMEs or sponsors. Always thank them for their help. Their jobs are tough, too. Give little gifts as you go.

- It's not about you, it's about the learner. There's a person out there working for your company who needs you to help him or her—and you can. Everything else is noise, so don't let it get to you.

- Change is constant. Don't just say it, believe it. Look for it. Thrive on it.

- When everything is chaos, keep it simple and enjoyable. For example, instead of a complex, software-based simulation, consider one with Post-it notes and markers that smell like fruit. You'll notice my supply lists are simple and lean, giving me speed and agility and fun.

For more on project management, check out my book *Project Management for Trainers* (2000, ASTD). Project management is a core competency for a performance consultant.

Onward!

So, what are you waiting for? No doubt you have a few messages on your phone and emails in your inbox asking for your help right now! Here's one of my favorite quotations to help get you going: "Enable me to teach with vision, for I help to shape the future. Empower me to teach with love, for I help to shape the world" ("A Teacher's Prayer," author unknown).

Teaching has evolved, and so too must we. Thank you for joining me on this adventure.

chapter 2

Basic Knowledge

Ways People Learn and Good Project Management

Before you can begin to implement fast, cheap, and great training triage, you need to have a basic understanding of

- how people learn
- how to manage complex projects
- how to create a learning environment
- your role in the intervention.

Because these interventions are so intense and compressed, it is critical that each participant learn more with less effort. Positive learning experiences lower stress, reduce conflicts, and build trust. In contrast, ineffective learning increases stress, triggers blame, and challenges feelings of self-worth. The problems presented in the chapters of this book demonstrate the abundance of stress that already exists. It is important that your interventions don't exacerbate the stress problem.

This chapter will help you review, or learn for the first time, the latest research on how people learn. As you deliver these training interventions, you will learn how to adapt the materials on the spot to meet the specific needs of that time and place. This may involve throwing in some new learning activities or leaving some out, but one thing's for sure, these choices can only be made with a complete understanding of why they were there in the first place. For more detailed information on all the topics in this chapter, refer to my 1999 book *The Accelerated Learning Fieldbook*.

How People Learn

There are two basic ways to think about the diversity of each individual learner. Learners have different preferences when it comes to receiving new information (intake) and then processing that information (multiple intelligences). Hermann International's research on brain dominance and Daniel Goleman's research into emotional intelligence and the emotional quotient (EQ) are also pertinent. In this book, you'll learn to audit your session flow using multiple intelligences to ensure consistency with brain dominance and EQ.

Intake Styles

In the field of neurolinguistic programming (NLP), studies on how individuals prefer to get new information into their heads have been conducted for years. Learning styles fall into three categories (visual, auditory, and kinesthetic) as shown in figure 2-1.

Each learner uses a combination of these three intake styles. Some fall clearly into one category, some have no preference between two, and some are equally able with all three. Intake styles are not the same as intelligence; whether you prefer to learn by seeing, hearing, or doing has no bearing on how intelligent you are. These styles just determine your preference for receiving new information. Talking about your intake preferences often leads to improved team communication.

It is easy to identify your own preference(s) and guess someone else's preference(s) from certain physical characteristics and behaviors. Visual learners prefer books or videos, tend to speak quickly in a somewhat high-pitched voice, look up when they are thinking, and say things like "I see what you mean." About 60 to 72 percent of the population prefers to learn this way.

Auditory learners prefer speeches, discussions, or tapes; speak slowly and quietly; look straight ahead when they are thinking; and use language like "I hear what you are saying." They make up between 12 and 18 percent of the population.

Finally, kinesthetic learners prefer to try something, speak quickly and with great changes in intonation and body language, look down when thinking, and use language like "I get it." Although across the general population, 18 to 30 percent prefer to learn kinesthetically, I have found that higher percentages of both kines-

Figure 2-1. Learning styles.

	Modality	Description	Average
	Visual	Intake by seeing	**60% to 72%**
	Auditory	Intake by hearing	**12% to 18%**
	Kinesthetic	Intake by doing	**18% to 30%**

thetic and auditory preferences are represented among the technical occupations than these averages suggest. Training people like you tend to be kinesthetic.

If you are trying to communicate something new to someone (as you will be in these interventions), you tend to communicate in the way you would like to be communicated to, reflecting your own preferences. For example, if you are a visual learner, you are likely to create beautiful graphics and fancy documents to communicate. If your client is an auditory learner, he or she doesn't want the picture; your client wants words—short and brief. This mismatch creates a barrier to communication and can often grow into conflict.

Instead, consider all three intake styles in everything you do. For example, when debriefing you can use active listening to summarize a response you heard; this tactic appeals to the auditory listeners in your audience. To reach out to those who prefer learning kinesthetically, write down your summary on a flipchart. Finally, if you write legibly so that the learner can actually *read* the response on the flipchart, you help the visual learners in the room.

In this book, the interventions have been designed to speak to all three types of intake styles as much as possible. Without fail, things that you have only spoken to the learners will be forgotten. How often have you told a class the page number you are on, only to have three or four people ask you "What page number is it?" By writing the page number on a flipchart and having learners turn to the page, you add kinesthetic and visual facets to the auditory, increasing the effect of simply hearing the information.

The Multiple Intelligences

Although intake styles reflect how people prefer to receive information, the intelligences reflect how people prefer to process information. The term was coined by Howard Gardner of Harvard University, who has been challenging the basic beliefs about intelligence since the early 1980s. Gardner initially described a list of seven intelligences:

- *interpersonal:* aptitude for working with others
- *logical/mathematical:* aptitude for math, logic, deduction
- *spatial/visual:* aptitude for picturing, seeing
- *musical:* aptitude for musical expression
- *linguistic/verbal:* aptitude for the written/ spoken word
- *intrapersonal:* aptitude for working alone
- *bodily kinesthetic:* aptitude for being physical.

In 1987, he added three additional intelligences to his list, but he expects that the list will continue to grow. The newer three intelligences are

- *emotional:* aptitude for identifying emotion (Goleman 1997, 2000, and 2002)
- *naturalist:* aptitude for being with nature
- *existential:* aptitude for understanding one's purpose.

Use activity 2-1 to help you think about your own multiple intelligences.

How do the different intelligences affect learning? Gardner believes that most people are comfortable in three or four of these intelligences and avoid the others. If you are not comfortable working with others, doing group case studies may interfere with your ability to process new material. Video-based instruction is not good for people with lower spatial/visual aptitudes. People with strong bodily/kinesthetic aptitudes need to move around while they are learning.

Learning energy comes from learning in a style that is best for the individual. Allowing your learners to use their own strengths and weaknesses helps them process and learn. Here's an example: Suppose you are debriefing one of the exercises. The exercise has been highly interpersonal (team activity), linguistic (plenty of discussion), spatial/visual (building an object with construction materials), musical (background music), logical/mathematical (rules and structure for activities) and kinesthetic (movement). You've honored all the processing styles except for intrapersonal. People need another exercise—debriefing—to allow them to reflect. Start by asking people to work quietly on their own, writing down five observations of the activity. Then ask them to share as an entire group.

Keep an eye on the multiple intelligences throughout the learning experience. If you're starting to feel the energy dragging, it usually means that people are exhausted by operating in an intelligence that is not best for them. Think about which intelligences have been neglected and get back to them.

Simply by realizing that people learn differently, you as facilitator can increase the amount of energy participants can invest in the intervention. Attention to learning techniques can turn classroom experiences into fun spots and speed learning in the process.

A Model for Learning Development

The situations that you find yourself in will most likely not be exactly like the ones I have described in subsequent chapters. You will have to adapt the approach, perhaps adding or removing materials. To do this, it is important that you follow a process that makes sure that you honor the way people learn. Use the Learner First Approach (seen in figure 2-2) to make these modifications.

These are the steps that make up the Learner First Approach:

1. *Identify the audience:* The first step is to define the audience to be influenced by the learning. This will help you determine how to adapt the course to the needs of your specific learners.

2. *Identify the learning need:* In this step, the course developer needs to determine what the business problem is that the company is trying to solve. Business reasons must drive learning objectives, and will help you prioritize the learning objectives for each session. Not only does this approach make the learning event easier to sell, it also ensures that the money being invested in

the learning event is a good return for the company. Clarity about the business problem also guarantees that the learners will analyze what information is need-to-know rather than merely nice-to-know.

3. *Create learning objectives:* Although learning objectives are included with each variation of the interventions in this book, you may run into a situation in which you need additional learning objectives. Once the business reason is clear and the needs are understood, the learning objectives can be created by clearly stating the audience and the behavior you will be able to observe during the learning event. The objectives provide guidance during the event for you to stay on track and within scope.

4. *Create exercises:* Even when the topic is running an effective meeting instead of climbing a mountain, people learn best when they try it themselves. You will notice that the sessions described in this book are combinations of exercises, simulations, and facilitation. You may find situations where you need to add or remove activities to reinforce new learning objectives.

Figure 2-2. The Learner First Approach.

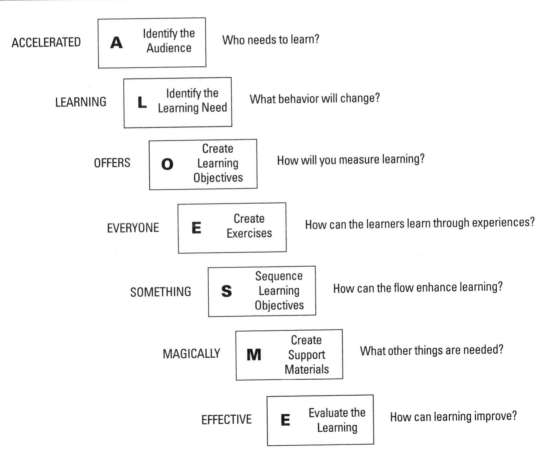

Source: Adapted from Russell, L. (1999). *The Accelerated Learning Fieldbook.* San Francisco: Jossey-Bass, 1999; Russell, L. (2001). *Project Management for Trainers.* Alexandria, VA: ASTD; and Shackelford, W. (2002). *e-Learning Project Management.* Alexandria, VA: ASTD, 2002.

5. *Sequence the learning objectives:* The fifth step of the Learner First Approach is to figure out the order in which you should cover the learning objectives and sequence the learning activities. There is a sense or intuition about sequencing that comes from experience in the medium that you are developing within. The sequencing for this leadership material has already been done for you.

6. *Create support materials:* The next to the last step of the Learner First Approach is to determine the materials you need to support the activity so that the learning objectives are achieved. Many of these have been provided for you with this book. Don't be afraid to mix and match activities from different chapters if that is what it takes to meet the needs of your customers.

7. *Evaluate the learning:* The final step of the Learner First Approach is to continually monitor and make changes based on the successes—or weaknesses—of the learning event over its lifetime.

How to Manage Complex Projects

As you prepare to implement your learning events, good project management can make the difference between success and failure. There are many details that need to be considered whenever a group of learners is assembled, and the order and timing is complex and critical. In this section, you will learn to dare to properly manage resources using my project management process (Russell, 2000).

Dare to Properly Manage Resources

Using the mnemonic "Dare to Properly Manage Resources," you can easily remember the phases, which correspond to the first letters of each of the words in the phrase Define, Plan, Manage, and Review. Look over figure 2-3 and reflect back on it as you read the overview of each aspect of this mnemonic.

Define answers the question, "Why does the business need this work done?"

- Identify what's within and what's outside the scope of the project.
- Identify how success will be measured.
- Identify constraints such as time, money, and resources.
- Identify the sponsor of the project.
- Identify the risk of the project, and think through contingency plans.

Plan answers the questions, "What will the project entail?" "Who will do the project?" and "How will the project get done?"

- Create a checklist/schedule for all the activities that need to be done before, during, and after the intervention.
- Figure out who will do each activity (probably you).
- Estimate how long each activity will take and plan your to-do list.

Manage answers the question, "How do we react to project glitches?"

- As the project begins, check your assumptions. Are all the answers from the Define phase still true?

- Adapt and change. Always be on the look out for new constraints or requirements.

- Communicate early and often with all people involved.

- Ask for help as needed.

Review answers the question, "What did we learn about projects?"

- When the project is over, think about what you did well and what could be improved next time.

Creating a Learning Environment

Research has shown that bland, neutral environments are so unlike the real world that learning achieved in these "sensory depravation chambers" cannot be transferred to the job. Color can be a powerful way to engage the limbic part of the brain and create long-term retention. It can align the right and left hemispheres of the brain. It can, however, trigger surprisingly negative emotions based on each person's history, culture, and preferences. Consider your use of color for specific things; for example, blue is the safest color to use for evaluations. Using a variety of primary colors for handouts, evaluations, and assessments, as well as Post-it notes and flipchart posters helps create an interesting, diverse environment.

Art work, plants, and pictures that help people feel comfortable and visually stimulated are also useful. Similarly, comfortable chairs and writing surfaces help people

Figure 2-3. The DARE approach.

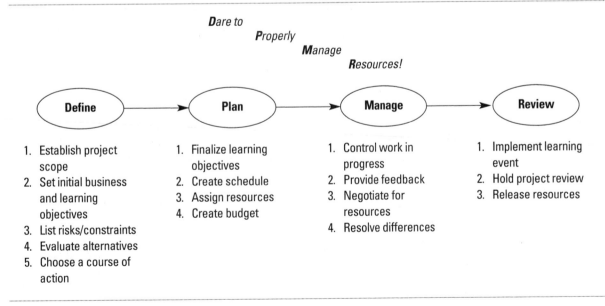

relax to learn. Because the complex business problems in these chapters often require reflection and role plays, consider seating that promotes individual reflection as well as group sharing. I prefer groups of three to five at round or square tables, with each chair positioned so that the screen can easily be seen. Leave plenty of room for each person, so that when he or she does need to reflect, the person feels he or she has some privacy.

Lots of flipcharts (one per table is wonderful if possible) with brightly colored markers creates a good interactive environment. Consider putting colorful hard candy on the tables, with bright cups of markers, pencils, and pens. I also like to bring a bag of sugar-free candy for the learners who prefer it. For the right level of trust to exist, your learners must feel as if they are welcome guests.

Play welcoming instrumental music as people come in, preferably copyright-free in a major key with a beat of about 80 beats per minute. (See Russell, 1999, for more on music use.) While learners are reflecting, play very quiet 60-beats-per-minute music. Play the same type of music while learners are in teams or working on exercises. Use lively music again when it is time for a break or lunch. Let music help you set an environment. Be careful to use music that is legal for classroom use—most is not.

Finally, you set the environment by your attitude. The way you greet people, your clothing, and your passion will all have a great effect on how learners respond to the learning atmosphere.

The Roles of Learning

Before you can help someone else learn, it is critical that you understand the values that you bring to your role as learning facilitator. You will find that you play all three roles if everything is going smoothly—trainer, facilitator, and learner. In addition, you are responsible for the logistics and process that ensure that everything comes together. To be successful as a learning facilitator, consider the following list:

- Learning is a gift to you from others and a gift from you to others.
- Choose carefully what you call yourself and what you call your outcome. I prefer the title learning facilitator over trainer.
- It's about the learners. As long as learning occurs, the intervention was a success. Don't get too attached to your agenda.
- You are part of the environment. Dress and behave in a way that is consistent with your role and your learning objectives.
- If you can't do it with passion, don't do it at all.

Learning and teaching are intimately connected. If you believe learning is limited, you limit your teaching. If you believe that to learn you must be in pain, you will teach with pain. If you believe that learning is liberating, your teaching will liberate others.

Figure 2-4 shows the changing roles you will juggle preparing for and delivering a learning event. When a class begins, you will play the role of trainer, bringing to the learning event a plan, structure, experience, and objectives. This will only be possible because you have a strong and reproducible logistics process. As you ask your learners to assign priorities to the objectives, you can slowly release control, inviting the learners to become partners in their own learning. As you move from the trainer role into the facilitator role, the objectives are the contract between the learners and the facilitator. Little by little, control is released to the learners.

Figure 2-4. Shifting among multiple roles based on a defined logistics process.

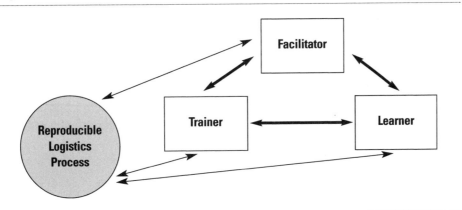

Sometimes the pendulum swings too far, and the learners begin to have so much fun that they start to move away from the learning objectives. This can shift the workshop flow toward entertainment rather than education—a mix sometimes called "edutainment." At this point, the learning facilitator must swing the pendulum back a bit, returning to the more control-oriented role of the trainer. Control is introduced just enough to ensure alignment with the learning objectives. Throughout the entire leadership workshop, you must balance flexibility (facilitation) and structure (training).

There is a third role that all great facilitators play in the classroom—the role of learner. If you are open to it, you can learn many new things whenever you are in class. If you believe that you have to be an expert as a learning facilitator, you will not be very effective. In short, you must be open-minded and receptive to your attendees.

Debrief

In this chapter, you learned about the knowledge and skills necessary to set the stage for your learners to explore real business problems, issues that are at crisis level. By honoring the unique learning profiles of your different learners; by following a clean, reproducible process to develop material; by managing the learning event project efficiently; and, finally, by creating an optimal learning environment, you can jump-start your own ability to foster learning among those whom you serve.

Activity 2-1. Identify your multiple intelligences.

For each aptitude, choose the three or four you feel are your strongest. Also select the ones you presently use most often at work and in your personal life.

☐ Interpersonal   ☐ Intrapersonal

☐ Logical/mathematical   ☐ Bodily/kinesthetic

☐ Spatial/visual   ☐ Emotional

☐ Musical   ☐ Naturalist

☐ Linguistic/verbal   ☐ Existential

Activity 2-1

chapter 3

Leadership

Stop and Grow Leaders

An executive from a U.S. Department of Defense consulting company called and requested leadership training. As a good performance consultant, you immediately think "red flag." You know from experience that a customer asking for leadership training can mean anything from a brief video to a multiyear learning experience. The first thing you have to do is find out what is the *true* problem that this executive needs to solve.

What They Say—The Situation

You: What happened that triggered this call?

Executive: Well, our consulting business unit has been very successful and profitable, but we are missing out on repeat business. The consultants doing the work are real technical experts, but they're not great at letting us know when they hear of new business opportunities at the client site. They aren't very comfortable with communication and don't think like salespeople. Because of this, we have missed out on some business that we could have easily won because we didn't hear about it until the sales staff made a call much later. Our salespeople can't be there all the time and our consultants are, so we'd like them to show more leadership in looking for additional work.

You: So, it sounds like you would like to enhance the consultant's ability to identify new opportunities and let the salespeople know about them. Are there any other issues that are slowing sales?

Executive: Actually, now that you ask, the other problem we have with new consultants is retention. They are so valuable technically, and it's a huge setback that we're having trouble keeping them. We've asked them what would make them stay, and most would like more communication and coaching from headquarters and their leaders. In our business, it is sometimes necessary for consultants to operate separate from their supervisors; however, new consultants often leave because they don't feel like they are a part of the company without a relationship and more communication with their boss. The problem is that the boss is also a consultant working at a different customer site, so finding time for communication with the people who report to them is difficult.

You: So, you would like the supervisors to show more leadership by coaching the consultants more effectively. You would also like all the consultants to prospect for new sales opportunities as part of their work at a customer's site.

Executive: Yes, that's it. In fact, we have put in our annual report to our stockholders that we are going to hold these leadership sessions for our senior consultants this year to address these two sales barriers. The pressure is on. That means that we have less than 8 months to do what we said we would do. I need the leadership program to start during this quarter!

What You Hear

Your conversation with the client and your research has brought you to the conclusions presented in table 3-1.

What You Do

Based on your conversation with the executive and your keen analytical skills, you agree to some key goals. First you identify two goals of the leadership program, the first of which is to increase sales by improving the consultants' ability

Table 3-1. Logical conclusions.

What the Client Says	What You Hear
The client requests a specific type of training.	I think I need training to solve this business problem. Are there other things that need to be done as well? Will you help me figure out my choices?
Consultant retention is the problem.	Retention is the problem, but I'm not clear what is causing the problem, though we have made some assumptions from some informal feedback.
The consultants don't know how to communicate or lead.	I assume it's a lack of communication and people skills, but it might have other causes like incentive, workload, etc.

to identify new business, pursue it initially, and then bring in the salespeople when appropriate. The other goal is to reduce consultant turnover by teaching experienced managers to coach new consultants more effectively. Then, to address the communication issues, you agree that initially your program will be targeted to senior consultants who have people reporting to them with the goal of rolling out a similar program (without the coaching component) to less-senior consultants later in the year.

Begin where all good performance solutions begin: Ask the right questions. Your training and performance instincts have already given you some good guidance, but like all successful interventions, you first have to figure out what's really behind that which is said. Here are some questions that need to be asked before the solution can be proposed:

- What types of behavioral changes would you like to see after the program is completed? What would make one of the senior consultants a good leader?

- How are consultants currently reimbursed for identifying sales opportunities? What is their incentive to turn new leads over to the salesforce? Are there any factors that would discourage them for turning over new leads, for example, workload, trust in the salesforce, and so forth?

- Whom could I talk to that is a new consultant about the challenges of staying with the company? Are there any consultants who have left whom I could talk to? Do you have any data through employee surveys that indicate that the supervisors (senior consultants) are not spending enough time with their new consultants?

- How are senior consultants compensated for coaching time? What incentives are provided for them to do the coaching? Because these senior consultants are consulting at a customer's site at the same time they are supervising people at other locations, what would prevent them from spending enough time with the new people? Does their job description indicate what percentage of their time should be spent on coaching?

- What is the industry average for retention of highly technical—and marketable—consultants? What is the goal for this company?

Results of Questions

When you are asking these questions, it is important to analyze the answers given to you by the employer; often, you may have to remove bias and infer the real answers to your questions. Based on the answers given to you, you have learned from asking these questions that:

- There is no incentive for consultants to sell through an account, and their workload prevents them from paying much attention to anything other than the work at hand. The company is currently considering a bonus for referrals and wants to emphasize this over trying to close sales themselves.

- The senior consultants rarely see their new consultants and, as one put it, "If they need something, I assume they'll email me."

- There is a tremendous cultural pressure for all consultants to log billable hours over everything else, including coaching.

- Senior consultants do have clear job descriptions regarding supervision and are expected to do coaching 25 percent of their time. The company is considering a bonus for each supervisor when a new consultant hits 1 year of service with successful results.

What Are the Project Constraints?

The employer of the company will also provide you with constraints and parameters within which your program must come together. You have learned that for this project the constraints include:

- An executive overview session must be delivered in 2 months.

- The senior leadership session must be delivered in 3 months and be completed within 6 months.

- Training for the senior consultants will take place on weekends to avoid conflicting with billable hours.

Your Triage Intervention

Now you are ready to propose your solution. The plan includes the following (figure 3-1):

- Prerequisite 360-degree leadership competency assessments and behavioral assessments for each participant. **Purpose:** Establish individual competency gaps and team behavioral gaps.

- An executive 1-day demo (review) of the initial 2-day leadership class including assessments. **Purpose:** Establish buy-in, set roles and process for ongoing reinforcement.

- Two 2-day sessions with homework (coaching, reading, performance review). **Purpose:** Allow tools and techniques practice and application and create a learning support group (other attendees).

- Ongoing review and fine-tuning for rollout to all other consultants.

You only have 4 weeks to build the initial executive session, then 4 weeks after that to roll out the initial class for the first participants. Here are more details about the four elements of your solution.

1. 360-Degree Leadership Assessments

Prerequisite 360-degree leadership competency assessments and behavioral assessments are used for each participant so that the senior consultants will have an accurate perspective of their own strengths and weaknesses. The 360-degree leadership competency assessment will tell each senior consultant how they are perceived by the people who work for them, their peers, and their boss. It will

Figure 3-1. Your leadership intervention.

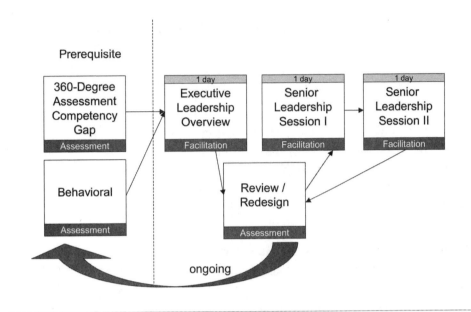

also provide you as course developer with overall learning gaps for the group that you can use to prioritize classroom time. A Web assessment would be preferable to make it easier to do and summarize.

The executive will prioritize what competencies are most important to assess. You provide a standard list (Russell, 2002) of competencies from which he may select. Executives often avoid 360-degree assessments simply because they dread spending months arguing about which competencies to include. It's much more practical to pick from an existing list, and, of course, such a list can save thousands of hours and dollars for the company.

You decide to use a DISC and values assessment to help each senior consultant understand their behavioral strengths as well as what motivates them. This will help them figure out ways to get help for work that presents challenges or causes them stress because of the level of effort required. You decide to use your own Quick 'n' Dirty versions in the classroom, rather than as a prerequisite. You hope to get the funding to do complete commercial versions by the second classroom session after proving the worth.

2. Executive 1- and 2-Day Leadership Classes

All of the senior managers and other managers who supervise senior consultants will attend a 1-day version of the initial 2-day leadership class. The purpose will be to familiarize them with what their staff will hear and be expected to do, as well as get their buy-in to the rollout. They will do the behavioral and values assessments but not the 360-degree assessments. The 1-day session will be highlights of topics, and many of the exercises of the senior consultants' 2-day sessions will be eliminated because of time constraints.

3. Two 2-Day Sessions With Homework

The senior consultants, handpicked by the executives, will attend a 2-day session. The content will be dictated by the results of the 360-degree leadership competency assessment, but will have a heavy emphasis on understanding and leveraging personal strengths in customer relationships, coaching, and supervising. The 360-degree leadership competency assessment will be a prerequisite to this workshop. After the workshop, the senior consultants will be asked to implement a coaching plan for their staff.

The second 2-day session will review the results of the coaching plan and drill down into more advanced coaching techniques. Again, this session will be driven by the priorities of the initial 360-degree leadership competency results. You believe this will involve more work on dealing with conflict, negotiating, and difficult coaching situations based on your discussions so far, but you won't know for sure until the results are in.

4. Review and Fine-Tune for Next Group

After the second 2-day session, you will review the behavioral results with the senior consultants and supervisors. A new plan will be built to determine what the next steps will be for the other consultants if necessary.

What You Build

The plan is approved, and now it is time for you to design the measurable learning objectives for each part of the proposed solution, determine facilitation requirements, and create course materials. Here are the details:

Prework:

- A Quick 'n' Dirty 360-Degree Assessment
- A Quick 'n' Dirty Behavioral Assessment

Classwork:

- Personal Vision: Who am I? Why am I here?
- Chunking: A Coaching Experience
- Coaching Role Play: Guardian Angels

Prework

Quick 'n' Dirty 360-Degree Assessment

Learning Objectives. After completing this assessment, each participant will be able to identify his or her own strengths and weaknesses as seen through the eyes of his or her staff, peers, and boss.

Required Equipment and Supplies. Paper forms or a Web-based assessment are required for the assessment in addition to an email notification. Finally, you must be able to track email reports to make sure assessments are done on time and print out result reports.

You can plug these competencies into a purchased 360-degree application, use one available in a Web application such as www.surveymonkey.com, or even do the surveys using email or paper. The choice depends on your budget and the number of survey participants. A 360-degree assessment on paper is best limited to 20 participants, with five or fewer people assessing the participants. It will take between 3 and 5 hours to summarize the data given this number of assessments. A Web-based 360-degree assessment with reporting offers unlimited scalability for an estimated cost of $150 USD per person. The choice is yours.

A 360-degree assessment is most effective when the supervisor, peers, staff, and self-assessments are summarized both separately and as a whole for comparison. Obviously, the more responses, the better the results will be. It is critical to ensure two things. First, the results must remain completely anonymous, with the exception of the boss, because in general there is only one boss entry. The person getting the results will not know which people entered which ratings. The second important factor is that the language asking them for their role (supervisor, peer, staff, self) is *very* clear. If participants choose the wrong role, it makes the results difficult to draw conclusions from.

Step-By-Step Design. The first thing you must do is determine the appropriate people to select the competencies (as can be done with activity 3-1). Once the competencies are selected, design the 360-degree questions. In this case, the executive requesting this program will make these choices.

Send the 360-degree instrument to each participant along with a letter or email for them to use to invite others to participate. (Activity 3-2 is a sample letter.) It is important that the participant request participation, not the course developer or facilitator.

It is necessary to be specific about the date the assessment will close. Track the number of assessments done a week before the assessment is closed and ask the leadership participant to email reminders to the people who have not yet completed their assessment. This way you are sure to get a sufficient number of assessments completed before the classes.

Once you have all the data, distribute the reports and report instructions. Then, use the cumulative results to prioritize the learning objectives for the instructor-led aspects of the leadership program.

Tips. Include a question for each competency asking the importance of that competency to the leadership participant's job. This way, if someone gives the leadership participant a lower ranking on a competency but also indicates that this is not a useful competency, there is not as a great a need to focus on closing the gap.

Roll assessments up from each sub-competency to major competency to show more actionable gaps. Be sure always to include instructions on how to read the reports when 360-degree reports are sent to participants, especially if you will not be able to explain them in person, to avoid misinterpretation.

Top Priority

In this case, you are going to distribute the 360-degree results in the first 2-day session via these steps:

1. Ask each person to read through his or her reports silently.

2. Ask each participant to pick one strength and one weakness.

3. Break into small groups (between three and five participants in each) to share thoughts.

4. Ask each person to share an example or story of a specific time when he or she succeeded because of a strength. Ask the team to help brainstorm why the situation went well.

5. Similarly, have them share an experience when they struggled because of their selected weakness. Ask the team to help brainstorm other ways the situation could have been handled.

6. Ask each leadership participant to create an individual development plan (activity 3-3), further clarifying their strengths, weaknesses, and actions to close the gaps between the two over time.

Results. The executive chooses eight leadership competencies from the list you gave him, and you implement a Web-based 360-degree leadership competency assessment based on this. You ask the executive to send out an email that you have helped write inviting the senior consultants to participate in this leadership program, which will begin with this 360-degree assessment. The email also contains dates that assessments are due, how to pick whom to ask to do the assessment, and a high level overview of the entire program. It also shares the dates for the two 2-day sessions, so they will know in advance not to make other plans.

At first, people do not get many assessments in, but you persist with email reminders. Eventually the data is complete, well within the timeframe. The results show three overwhelmingly common gaps:

- The senior consultants do not feel competent in their role as coaches, and their staff does not feel as if they are coached well.

- All staff felt that people above them did not listen to them.

- All staff felt that it was the supervisors' job to translate the company vision into action but this was not being done. Most consultants felt unsure how what they did aligned with the company vision and strategy.

Quick 'n' Dirty Behavioral Assessment

In this example, a behavioral and motivation assessment (DISC and PIAV) was done for each of the participants. Using these full profiles provides each leadership participant with the following:

- clarity about his or her preferred behaviors including his or her concern for tasks, people, urgency, and diligence

- clarity about his or her adapted behaviors—how differently the participant is behaving from his or her preferred behaviors

- clarity about his or her motivators—what kinds of things are engaging and what things are distasteful.

Figure 3-2 provides Quick 'n' Dirty versions of DISC and PIAV to use as a rapid, inexpensive option. Only use these versions as a last resort; the full versions provide much stronger learning and business returns.

In our story we found that many of the senior consultants preferred completing tasks carefully—even perfectly. They were drawn to situations where they could learn new things and had a tendency to measure success through income. The assessments also revealed that a majority of the senior consultants were not "people" people; they just did not feel comfortable one-on-one. Last, some of these senior consultants were not comfortable in their roles as coach, causing great stress to all concerned.

Learning Objectives. Each participant will learn about his or her own strengths and weaknesses as seen through behavior and motivation personal assessments.

Required Equipment and Supplies. You need to provide paper forms or Web-based assessments and instructions for interpreting the assessment results. A prerequisite assessment is used so that the upcoming leaders in your session will have a personal perspective about their own strengths and weaknesses. It also provides the facilitator with an understanding of the underlying factors creating some of the problems identified by the training sponsors.

Figure 3-2. Quick 'n' Dirty versions of DISC and PIAV.

HOW you behave: DISC

C / D / S / I

Careful	Urgent
Objective, clear	Pioneering
High standards	Innovative
Good analyst	Driven
Detailed	Likes challenge
Picky	Demanding
Aloof	Quick to anger
Fearful	

Steady and sincere	Optimistic
Patient	Motivator
Empathetic	Team player
Logical	Problem solver
Service-oriented	Emotionally needy
Apathetic under stress	Inattentive
Passive	Trusting
Resists change	Poor with details

WHY you behave: PIAV

Traditional / Theoretical / Utilitarian / Individualistic / Aesthetic / Social

Search for value of life
Champion of beliefs
Rigid
Order, unity
Always right

Help others
Empathy
Generous
Self-sacrifice
Can't say "no"
Stop hate and conflict

Seeks truth/ knowledge
Problem solving
Impractical
Watches "Discovery Channel," PBS

Achieve inner vision
Self-fulfillment
Humor or sarcasm
Impractical
Inner feelings not logic

Make money
Practical
Future oriented, savings
Workaholic
Never enough

Seeks to win
Control, power
End justifies means
Breaks rules
Can appear to feel superior to others

Audience. Each leadership participant will do these two assessments. We have found that it is critical to ensure people that the results will remain completely anonymous. Assessment results should never be shared with anyone other than the person they concern, unless permission is given in advance. In addition, let your participants know that good assessments are very difficult to "mess around with." The results are generally accurate, but never exact.

Step-by-Step. Distribute the assessments to participants. If possible, you should do this before you spend time together. You need to be specific about the date the assessment will close. Track the number of assessments done a week before the assessment is closed and remind the people who have not yet completed their assessment. The next phase is to distribute reports and report instructions. Finally, use the cumulative results to prioritize the learning objectives for the instructor-led aspects of the leadership program.

Tips. Encourage each participant to be open to the results, even if they do not seem exactly right. I have found that the people who are most bothered by the results have the most to discover, but require you to have great patience and gentleness.

Top Priority

Whether debriefing as a group or one-on-one, follow these steps:

- Ask each person to read through his or her reports silently, preferably before the face-to-face time.

- Ask each participant to pick one strength and one weakness.

- If working as a team, break into small groups of three to five participants to share thoughts.

- In either a team or one-on-one setting, ask each person to share an example of a specific time when he or she succeeded because of a strength. Ask the team to help brainstorm why the situation went well.

- In either a team, or one-on-one, ask each person to share an instance when he or she struggled because of the weakness chosen. Ask the team to help brainstorm other ways the situation could have been handled.

- Now ask each leader to think of people they have difficulty communicating with. Could it be a behavioral or motivation difference? How can that be addressed?

- Ask each leadership participant to create an individual development plan (see activity 3-3) clarifying further their strengths, weaknesses, and actions to close the gaps in the future.

Classwork

Personal Vision: Who Am I? Why Am I Here?

In this example, each participant created a vision for his or her role at the company. The results showed that some consultants did not see themselves as part of the sales process, and often consultants restricted their role to the implementation of a technology, rather than the solving of a customer need.

Learning Objectives. Each participant will come up with his or her own description of the role he or she plays at the company, and then the group will come to a consensus.

Required Equipment and Supplies. You will need flipcharts, markers, and stickers for voting if you choose to use them.

This facilitation technique is used to create a discussion around why consultants are important to the company. It is always interesting how different people see their roles. The wide variance in responses may really surprise the participants. This is especially useful when you are hoping to help people see the role they play in serving the needs of the company's customers. In our case, we were also concerned about the role played in serving the needs of newer consultants.

Step-by-Step. Make sure each participant has blank paper and something to write with, and then proceed to tell them the following story:

> Imagine that you are at a party with some people who you do not know very well. One of these people asks you where you work and what you do. You explain it to the best of your ability. Suddenly, they ask you, "Why do you work there? What is it about your job that you like so much that you get up every day and do it?"

Instruct the participants to begin to answer the question using three verbs and one noun. For example, "I promote, market, and sell products," would be a sufficient yet succinct answer to the question with which they were presented. It is also fine to add descriptive words if necessary. The sentence, "I promote, market, and sell technology products to grocery stores," would be a suitable, slightly more descriptive answer to the question.

Give participants 10 minutes to think about their own answers. Then, you should encourage them to get into groups of three to five people and share their answers. Give them another 10 minutes to come up with a statement consisting of three verbs and one noun that they all agree with. Ask them to write it on a flipchart page when they are in agreement.

As a large group, discuss the different meanings of each of the statements. Give everyone 10 stickers (or use colored markers). Explain to them that they each have 10 votes to cast on the words they like the best out of all the flipchart entries. Using the stickers (or checkmarks using the markers), they will individually choose their favorite verbs and nouns from the entries. They can spread the votes any way they want—they can put all 10 votes on one verb they feel strongly about, or put one vote on six verbs and four nouns. Give people 5 minutes to vote.

Identify the statement that received the most votes overall. Post it on the wall and refer back to it throughout the ongoing leadership discussions to reinforce learning.

Tips. Consider some of these ideas to get the ball rolling:

- Use purchased stickers that look like dollar bills, so voting really seems like spending money. Check out www.photostamps.com to create stickers of just about anything you want.

- Keep the focus on the message that the people want to communicate and away from a particular word or logistics debate. What's important is that the words you use to describe yourself dictate your behavioral choices.

- You will probably have to explain the voting technique multiple times using examples. This is a tough, nonlinear concept for some people at first.

Top Priority

When debriefing the group, follow these steps:

- Compare verbs and/or nouns two at a time, for example, how is customer different as a noun than product? How would your job look differently?

- If you have already discussed the behavioral and 360-degree assessments, integrate these into the debriefing. Which words show more sense of urgency? Which words indicate a focus on making money? Which statements seem to include coaching (or a competency that was overall weak in the group's 360-degree assessment)?

- It is important to follow the steps so that each individual gets the opportunity to think first by him- or herself, then with a small group, and then as a collective. This gives them the safety and trust to investigate and try out new thoughts.

Chunking: A Coaching Experience

In this example, we use a game developed by the famed game master Thiagi (www.thiagi.com). It's an exercise called Chunking to catch people in their default coaching behaviors. Coaching was emphasized because of the results of the 360-degree assessment, however, I have not done a leadership session yet where coaching was not a developmental goal. The results of this game and discussion showed the emerging leaders that they:

- Tend to *tell* instead of *ask* when in a coaching situation.

- Feel obligated to help a bit too much, rather than grow the person they are helping.

- Very few think to ask the person being coached how much help he or she wants! The coach almost always decides for the person.

Learning Objectives. Each participant will learn about his or her own coaching strengths and weaknesses by either participating as an observer, a person being coached, or a coach.

Required Equipment and Supplies. You should provide a sufficient number of flipcharts and markers depending on the group size you will be working with. In addition, you need to provide a set of Chunking worksheets that include the Chunking game handout (activity 3-4), the hint worksheet (activity 3-5), the answer handout (activity 3-6), and an observation sheet (activity 3-7) that will help organize participants' thoughts at the conclusion of the game.

Audience. All participants will be involved in this exercise and will play either the role of coach, person being coached, or observers.

Step-by-Step. Break the room into teams of four to five people. Determine the roles each person will play by the following rules:

1. The person with the most children will play the role of the coach (pets can be the tie breaker).

2. The person with the least years of service with the company will play the role of the person being coached.

3. All remaining people will be observers. Explain that observers will take out paper and writing utensils, and observe the coach and person being coaching, noting behaviors, phrases/language, emotions, success/failures used throughout the roleplay. They should also note what goes well and what could be improved. However, observers cannot help or speak during the activity.

4. Finally, ask each of the coaches to come up to the front for some private instructions from you. At this time, you will pass out the hint and answer handouts quickly with very little discussion. If they ask you if they can tell the person the answer, tell them they can do whatever they want.

5. Pass out the Chunking worksheet and explain how to solve the puzzle. Give each team 10 minutes to solve the puzzle.

Tips. There are a few things you can do during the activity to maximize the learning experience. First, resist the temptation to say more than you need to: the fewer instructions the better. You are trying to catch people in suboptimal coaching behaviors. You should also monitor the room to ensure that observers are observing rather than helping. (It is really hard to stay out of it.) Last, try to capture some language to share during debrief as you wander around. Observe emotions and look for language that expresses that emotion.

Top Priority

Debrief using the following process:

- Ask each person to write down at least one thing that went well, and one thing that could be improved in the coaching exercise.

- Ask the observers to share their answers first and place them on the flipchart pages with which you've provided each group.

- Ask the person being coached to share his or her answers, and add them to the list.

- Finally, ask the coaches to share their answers.

- Announce to the group that the coaches had the answers all along. Ask the coaches why they did or didn't give the answers to the person being coached. Ask the people coached how they feel about the fact that the coach did or did not give them the answer. Why did this happen? Stress the importance of a coaching session being driven by the *unique* needs of the person being coached.

- Ask each leadership participant to create an individual development plan (look back to activity 3-3), clarifying further his or her strengths, weaknesses, and actions to close the gaps in the future around coaching.

Coaching Role Play: Guardian Angels

Use this coaching role play after the Chunking exercise. This way, participants have an opportunity to practice the behaviors they have just learned and have some success.

Learning Objectives. Each participant will learn about his or her own strengths and weaknesses as a coach and will have an opportunity to try on new behaviors in a safe practice setting.

Required Equipment and Supplies. You need to provide role-play scenario worksheets (activities 3-8 and 3-9) in addition to the standard flipcharts and markers to aid the visual learners.

Audience. All participants will take a turn acting as a coach, the person being coached, and a guardian angel to one of the two.

Step-by-Step. This role play is designed to encourage misconceptions and poor judgments from both the coach and the coached, so be sure to keep an eye out for these behaviors.

1. Pass out the instructions for the role play. Give everyone a few minutes to read through the scenario.

2. Break into teams of four to five participants each. Ask for one volunteer from each team to be the coach first. Ask for one other volunteer from each group to be the coach's guardian angel. Their job will be to help the coach prepare for the coaching session, and, at any time during the role play, the coach can freeze the action to get help from the guardian angel.

3. Ask for one of the remaining team members to volunteer to be the person being coached. The others will be his or her guardian angels. Distribute a role-play scenario to them (either activity 3-8 or 3-9). Give everyone 5 minutes to prepare.

4. Begin the role play in each team and let it go on for approximately 10 minutes.

5. Debrief using the instructions in the next "Top Priority" section.

6. Ask each team to make a list of what went well and what could be improved.

7. Debrief as an entire class, and ask each group to share one lesson they learned during the role play. Capture these on a flipchart.

8. Rotate the couple who played the coach person and the coach's guardian angel to a new group where they will be the coached person and his or her guardian angel. The others in the new group will now play the role of the coach with the second role-play roles (either activity 3-8 or 3-9, whichever you did not use in the last scenario).

9. Debrief in the same way.

Tips. Be very careful to keep this a positive experience. It will be hard for some people and stressful, but the guardian angels should be a big help. Keep emphasizing the importance of learning from the experience.

Changing behavior is very hard because people don't always see their own behavior clearly. Continue to talk about how the participants will notice ways to adapt their own behaviors to the needs of someone else and that each coaching situation is unique.

Top Priority

Whether debriefing as a group or in a one-on-one situation, follow these steps:

- Ask each person to think about what went well and what could have been improved in the coaching role play. Individually, have each person write down three ideas for each category if he or she can.

- Have each person at each table share his or her three "what went well" and "improvements," one person at a time. Ask someone at the table to accumulate a list. Start with the observers and finish with the coach and his or her guardian angel.

- Bring everyone back together, and ask each team, in turn, to share one thing that went well and one area of improvement that no one else has said yet. Accumulate these on a flipchart at the front of the room.

- Repeat for additional role plays.

- Ask each leadership participant to create an individual development plan (activity 3-3), further clarifying his or her strengths, weaknesses, and actions to close the gaps in the future.

Customizing Tips. First, ask the participants instead of the executives, or both, to choose the competencies ahead of time. If there is no time or buy-in to do the assessment as prework, use the 360-degree assessment with only the people in the room at the start of the session. Note, however, that this will only work if people know each other fairly well. The other caveat is that the prework is difficult to distribute, and people may be too busy or lack the trust to participate. Be clear with all the executives how essential this data is and use their clout to get the assessments done.

It is critical that the CEO (or someone else with great power and respect) kicks off the classes or at least is responsible for inviting the emerging leaders through an email or letter before the session.

The executives must not only review the classes but also take them. Taking a class means they do all the exercises and live the experience so that they can support their learners more fully. It is critical that at least one of the executives attends as a student in each instructor-led class. At a minimum, an executive can attend as a guest speaker and share his or her own leadership challenges to model high-level buy-in and support.

Carry the vision exercise results from the executives' overview into the class with the participants. Comparing these two "answers" can create powerful discussion and learning opportunities.

Measuring Your Success

There are multiple difficulties measuring the return-on-investment (ROI) of leadership initiatives. First of all, measuring the growth in competencies (which can be done with another 360-degree assessment after a period of time) does not necessarily indicate that business value has occurred. In addition, it can be misleading to measure a business indicator, in our case a growth in sales and a growth in retention, because there are many other external factors (such as the economy) that can affect the numbers. Also, measuring competencies or business indicators can only be done after enough time has passed to see results. Measuring competency improvement makes no sense unless at least six months have passed. Measuring business results usually takes between 12 and 18 months.

As dismal as this may look, there are some ways that measurements can be made. Using the email surveys (activity 3-2), ask stakeholders (executive sponsors, 360-degree assessment participants, and so forth) to subjectively evaluate the improvement for the business. You can also track the financial numbers from sales, retention, and similar measures that you established in the beginning as the goal. Detail the other factors that may have affected these numbers, both in the positive and negative.

In our story, building accountability and partnership had an expected and unexpected result. The consultants felt more a part of the company and, therefore, expressed ideas and complaints that they were hesitant to express prior to the program. The executives initially responded openly to these concerns, but were not able to finish the job. A key barrier was that consultants' pay and bonuses were tied to on-the-job hourly work, and when senior consultants spent time coaching new consultants, it cost them both money. The executives were not willing to change the incentives and job descriptions, so the change they desired did not occur.

Debrief

When you have an executive sponsor asking for training for people who think they don't have a problem, you have a special challenge. In this case, these were highly talented people and the business had not asked them to be great at consulting until this point. The use of 360-degree and behavioral assessments was the critical data needed to get buy-in from the learners. This way, the perception of the executive sponsor was not the only voice that the learners heard.

These types of problems, however, cannot be solved with just a training intervention. Without reworking the job roles, the compensation, and the processes as well as educating the upper management, the change of long-term improvement is very low.

In the next chapter, you will read about a situation that is much more time critical. What do you do when a project team just can't seem to work together and a new product rollout is failing because of the dynamics of the team?

Activity 3-1. 360-degree leadership assessment.

Relationship to the person being assessed (pick ONE):

☐ Self ☐ Supervisor ☐ Peer ☐ Subordinate

Rate the person being assessed in terms of each of the characteristics listed below by circling a number from 1 (indicating no skill in the characteristic) and 6 (perfect skills in the characteristic).

Self-understanding	
• Develop clarity of personal values, purpose, and vision	1 2 3 4 5 6
• Develop and execute a personal branding strategy	1 2 3 4 5 6
• Demonstrate authenticity through behavioral alignment with values and vision	1 2 3 4 5 6
• Accept responsibility for personal and leadership actions	1 2 3 4 5 6
• Know and trust own intuition	1 2 3 4 5 6
• Learn to learn: new technology	1 2 3 4 5 6
Resiliency	
• Be willing to jump in and get things started	1 2 3 4 5 6
• Seek opportunities for performance improvement and development	1 2 3 4 5 6
• Build off of others' ideas for the benefit of the decision	1 2 3 4 5 6
• Maintain appropriate, empowered attitude	1 2 3 4 5 6
• Persist in managing and overcoming adversity	1 2 3 4 5 6
• Act proactively in seeking new opportunities	1 2 3 4 5 6
• Prioritize tasks, manage time effectively	1 2 3 4 5 6
Interpersonal and Relationship Skills	
• Understand and appreciate diversity of perspective and style	1 2 3 4 5 6
• Participate and contribute fully as a team member	1 2 3 4 5 6
• Demonstrate empathy and understanding	1 2 3 4 5 6
• Build trust and demonstrate trustworthiness	1 2 3 4 5 6
Communication Skills:	
• Understand and adapt to your audience to help others learn	1 2 3 4 5 6
• Express intention clearly and concisely in written communications	1 2 3 4 5 6
• Build collaboration and clearly articulate intention in verbal communications	1 2 3 4 5 6
• Possess formal presentation skills	1 2 3 4 5 6
• Listen for understanding	1 2 3 4 5 6
• Manage flow of communication/information	1 2 3 4 5 6
Employee Development (Coach and Motivate)	
• Motivate employees to high performance	1 2 3 4 5 6
• Coach for development and improved performance	1 2 3 4 5 6
• Manage with appreciation/respect for diversity of individual values and needs	1 2 3 4 5 6
• Delegate tasks as needed and with awareness of employee development opportunities	1 2 3 4 5 6
• Select appropriate staff to fulfill specific project needs and responsibilities	1 2 3 4 5 6

Activity 3-1, page 1

Activity 3-1. 360-degree leadership assessment (continued).

Customer Orientation	
• Understand and apply customer needs and expectations	1 2 3 4 5 6
• Gather customer requirements and input	1 2 3 4 5 6
• Partner with customer in gathering requirements, maintaining communication flow, and managing work	1 2 3 4 5 6
• Set and monitor performance standards	1 2 3 4 5 6
Strategic Business Acumen	
• Demonstrate ability to ethically build support for a perspective you feel strongly about	1 2 3 4 5 6
• Take a holistic view by thinking in terms of the entire system and the effects and consequences of actions and decisions	1 2 3 4 5 6
• Operate with an awareness of marketplace competition and general landscape of related business arenas	1 2 3 4 5 6
• Possess general business acumen—functions of strategic planning, finance, marketing, manufacturing, research and development, and so on	1 2 3 4 5 6
Project Leadership	
• Build cohesive teams with shared purpose and high performance	1 2 3 4 5 6
• Set, communicate, and monitor milestones and objectives	1 2 3 4 5 6
• Gain and maintain buy-in from sponsors and customers	1 2 3 4 5 6
• Prioritize and allocate resources	1 2 3 4 5 6
• Manage multiple, potentially conflicting priorities across various and diverse disciplines	1 2 3 4 5 6
• Create and define systems and processes to translate vision into action	1 2 3 4 5 6
• Maintain an effective, interactive, and productive team culture	1 2 3 4 5 6
• Manage budget and project progress	1 2 3 4 5 6
• Gather and analyze appropriate data and input and manage "noise" of information overload	1 2 3 4 5 6
• Manage risk versus reward and return-on-investment equations	1 2 3 4 5 6
• Balance established standards with need for exceptions in decision making	1 2 3 4 5 6
• Align decisions with needs of business and organizational and team values	1 2 3 4 5 6
• Make timely decisions in alignment with customer and business pace	1 2 3 4 5 6
Creating and Actualizing Vision	
• Create a clear and inspirational vision of the desired outcome	1 2 3 4 5 6
• Align the vision with broader organizational strategies	1 2 3 4 5 6
• Translate the vision into manageable action steps	1 2 3 4 5 6
• Communicate vision to enroll/enlist staff, sponsors, and customers	1 2 3 4 5 6
• Influence and evangelize (sales, negotiation)	1 2 3 4 5 6
• Gather appropriate input	1 2 3 4 5 6
• Understand individual motivators and decision-making styles and utilize to enroll others	1 2 3 4 5 6
• Facilitate win/win solutions	1 2 3 4 5 6

Activity 3-1, page 2

Activity 3-1. 360-degree leadership assessment (continued).

Create, Support, and Manage Change	
• Able to undertake improvement initiatives (three levels: managing your own transition or transformation, managing a corporate (external) change initiative, coaching others through transition)	1 2 3 4 5 6
• Identify and implement appropriate change initiatives and efforts	1 2 3 4 5 6
• Promote and build support for change initiatives	1 2 3 4 5 6
• Understand cost-benefit and return-on-investment of change initiatives	1 2 3 4 5 6
• Manage transition with employees by guiding and supporting the change process	1 2 3 4 5 6
• Support staff in navigating transitional process and challenges through organizational change	1 2 3 4 5 6
• Demonstrate and build resilience in the face of change	1 2 3 4 5 6

Activity 3-1, page 3

Activity 3-2. Email invitation for 360-degree assessment.

Dear _____,

I am currently participating in a program to build my leadership competencies. To help me identify my strengths and challenges, I would appreciate your feedback. Attached is an assessment that I will be filling out myself and sending to my supervisor, my peers, and my subordinates. This will give 360-degree feedback on my leadership competencies.

I would appreciate it if you could take 10 minutes and provide me with your feedback. Please note that your feedback is anonymous and I will not know which results came from which person.

It is important that you select the role you play in your relationship with me (at the top— supervisor, peer, or subordinate) so that the report can be summarized for me.

Please email your response to yournamehere@somewhere.com by _____ [insert date] .

Sincerely,

Leadership Candidate

Activity 3-2

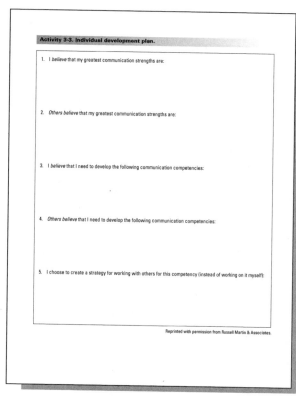

Activity 3-3. Individual development plan.

1. I *believe* that my greatest communication strengths are:

2. *Others believe* that my greatest communication strengths are:

3. I *believe* that I need to develop the following communication competencies:

4. *Others believe* that I need to develop the following communication competencies:

5. I choose to create a strategy for working with others for this competency (instead of working on it myself):

Reprinted with permission from Russell Martin & Associates.

Activity 3-3

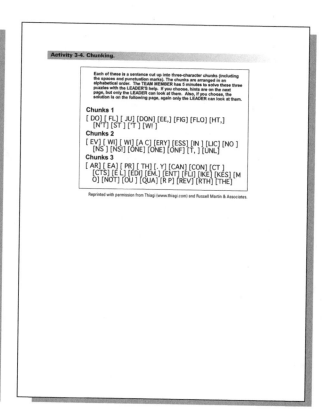

Activity 3-4. Chunking.

Each of these is a sentence cut up into three-character chunks (including the spaces and punctuation marks). The chunks are arranged in an alphabetical order. The TEAM MEMBER has 5 minutes to solve these three puzzles with the LEADER'S help. If you choose, hints are on the next page, but only the LEADER can look at them. Also, if you choose, the solution is on the following page, again only the LEADER can look at them.

Chunks 1
[DO] [FL] [JU] [DON] [EE,] [FIG] [FLO] [HT,] [N'T] [ST] ['T] [W!]

Chunks 2
[EV] [WI] [WI] [A C] [ERY] [ESS] [IN] [LIC] [NO] [NS] [NS!] [ONE] [ONE] [ONF] [T,] [UNL]

Chunks 3
[AR] [EA] [PR] [TH] [. Y] [CAN] [CON] [CT] [CTS] [E L] [EDI] [EM.] [ENT] [FLI] [IKE] [KES] [M O] [NOT] [OU] [QUA] [R P] [REV] [RTH] [THE]

Reprinted with permission from Thiagi (www.thiagi.com) and Russell Martin & Associates.

Activity 3-4

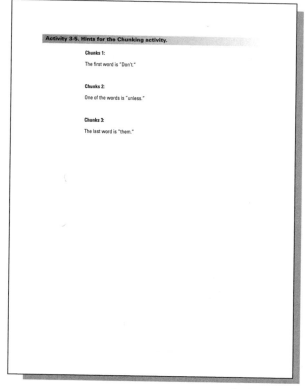

Activity 3-5. Hints for the Chunking activity.

Chunks 1:
The first word is "Don't."

Chunks 2:
One of the words is "unless."

Chunks 3:
The last word is "them."

Activity 3-5

Activity 3-6. Solutions for the Chunking activity.

Chunks 1: Don't fight, don't flee, just flow!

Chunks 2: In a conflict, no one wins unless everyone wins!

Chunks 3: Conflicts are like earthquakes. You cannot predict them or prevent them.

Activity 3-6

Activity 3-7. Coaching observation sheet for Chunking activity.

- What were some of the things that you think could have been improved by the coach?

- What were some of the things you thought the coach did well?

- Who talked the most doing this coaching session? How did this happen?

- Who directed the agenda of this coaching session? How could you tell?

- What did the coach tell the person being coached about having hints or the answer?

Activity 3-7

Activity 3-8. Manager role-play worksheet.

You are a very successful technical consultant, and because of your success you have been promoted to manager.

One of the "problems" you have inherited is an employee who is a highly gifted and accomplished technical consultant but has problems interacting with the customers. Recently, when a customer asked this consultant to pursue expanding the scope of the contract, the consultant refused, saying that he was already using up too much personal time.

To increase business, all consultants must learn to take similar sales opportunities and forward them to the sales organization. In this case, a different consultant might have been used to fulfill the needs of the customer if personal time was an issue. However, you just heard from the customer that the company has already hired another company to meet this need, and the entire account is being phased out. This is the first you heard of the issue; you have had no communication from the on-site consultant.

You have called a meeting with the consultant to discuss this account specifically but also to clarify measurable behavior changes for the future.

Activity 3-8

Activity 3-9. Consultant role-play worksheet.

You are a very successful technical consultant, and because of your success you have been given a very difficult customer to work with.

One of the "problems" you have inherited is that the customer constantly tries to slip additional scope into the project work that you have been assigned. You have done an excellent job keeping the requirements stable, which has allowed you to deliver impeccable quality. In addition, your time with your family is important to you and you defend it at all costs.

The company has recently been pushing the consultants to sell. You are not a salesperson, and have no desire to be one. If the salespeople in the company do not do their job, the consultants cannot be depended on to do sales as well as technical work. If this kind of pressure continues, you will take your technical prowess elsewhere.

Your boss has called a meeting with you, and you assume it is to congratulate you on the wonderful job you are doing with this customer.

Activity 3-9

chapter 4

Strategic Vision
No Time for Strategy

One of your key product managers calls. He is concerned because he is under pressure to deliver a new product on time. However, his team continues to seem unclear about the priorities and direction of this development. In addition, they don't seem to get along very well.

What They Say—The Situation

You: How long have you felt that the team was disconnected?

Executive: About 4 months ago I realigned my teams. This team is composed of two different groups from other projects. One of the projects was cancelled, and the other was finished although it had some issues. I had hoped putting these teams together would be an opportunity for them to emotionally recover from their bad histories. As people got to know each other, I expected there to be some delays, but they aren't becoming connected and it's gotten to the point where the project timeline is in jeopardy.

You: It seems like the individuals are having trouble recovering from their last project challenges. Maybe working on relationships with new team members is a challenge they don't feel ready for. What have you seen that would indicate this is the problem?

Executive: That's plausible. The two teams pretty much keep to themselves. In meetings, the original project teams always sit together and tend to criticize people's ideas from the other team more than those from their own. They don't seem to have a shared buy-in or even understanding of this project. How am I ever going to get them over this? I don't have time for them all to go to team building, and frankly, I've never seen great results from that sort of thing. Should I put them through a strategy class?

You: Let's decide first what you'd like to accomplish. What kind of behavior changes would you look for after a session with these teams?

Executive: I would like them to get along better, and learn to trust each other, not just the people on their original project teams. I'd like them to share information so that we can get this project done on time. I'd also like them to get over their last project so they can be enthusiastic about this mission-critical project.

What You Hear

Your conversation with the client and your research has brought you to the following conclusions laid out in table 4-1.

Table 4-1. Logical conclusions.

What the Client Says	What You Hear
Request for an unknown type of help.	I have a problem I have no idea how to fix. What kind of training could help me?
The team isn't getting along.	I guess I made a mistake when I put these two project teams together, but it's too late to start over with new people.
The team hasn't bought into this project.	I assume it is a lack of confidence after the last two projects, but I don't know how to get these two teams collaborating past that.

What You Do

You build agreement with the client that the goals of this program are to:

- improve the project velocity and success through a stronger team with shared vision, values, and strategy
- foster team collaboration
- reduce formation of cliques within the team.

The audience will be the team members on this project as well as the manager who is working with you.

You begin where all good performance solutions begin—with asking the right questions. Your training and performance instincts have already given you some good guidance, but you first have to figure out what's really behind what is said. Here are some questions that need to be asked before the solution can be proposed:

- How many people are really feeling the way the manager describes? Often, there are a few people with strong emotions who are influencing the others. Who are these people?

- What is the current vision of the project? What are the constraints? How is this current project so critical to the business?

- What kind of project plan exists now? What kind of role definitions?

- How much time can this team sacrifice away from the project?

- What happens specifically in project meetings? Where do people sit? Who are the people who speak out more than others?

Results of Questions

Assume you have learned from asking these questions that:

- There are two strong people, one from each original project team, who seem to be influencing the rest of the project team members. Others defer to these two.

- The project roles are unclear. The only thing documented well on this project is the looming deadline.

- When asked, different people talk about different project goals. One says that the project is quality driven, but another says that the project needs to be "quick and dirty."

- Everybody is working very hard and putting in many hours. In the absence of any measurable milestones, people are feeling overworked. The result is low morale.

What Are the Project Constraints?

There are two constraints on this initiative. First, the project work takes priority, but the project manager has agreed to three 2-hour sessions for 3 weeks in a row. In addition, the sessions need to begin as soon as possible, preferably next week.

Your Triage Intervention

You have proposed to the executive a plan, which he has accepted (figure 4-1).

Session 1

- As a prerequisite to the session, each participant must complete an individual learning history (activity 4-1). **Purpose:** Allow people to review their past project and share what they learned from that experience, both good and bad. This helps people vent and move into the future project.

- Participants will then attend a 2-hour session for sharing their learning histories. **Purpose:** Establish trust and point out project mistakes that may be recurring.

Figure 4-1. An intervention for building a team vision.

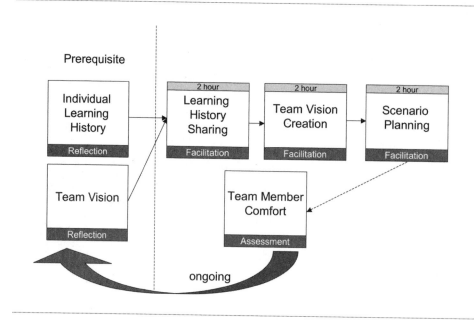

Session 2

■ Participants should develop a team vision containing three verbs and one noun as a prerequisite to the second session. **Purpose:** Allow people to express their view of the vision of the project without being influenced by the views of the influential, self-proclaimed leaders.

■ During the second 2-hour session, participants share their team vision, build consensus, and establish rules of engagement for their group's vision. **Purpose:** Continue to build trust and break down cliques within the old teams to create a common project vision and to develop rules of engagement to regulate team behavior themselves (activity 4-2).

Session 3:

■ The final 2-hour session will use scenario planning. **Purpose:** Help the entire team imagine four possible future states for the project and build a consensus action plan to move the project toward agreed-upon success (activity 4-3).

Better Get a Move on

You only have 1 week to get ready for the first session, and less than 5 days to prepare for each of the following two sessions. As you've thought the situation through more thoroughly, you come up with a more refined detailed plan. Here are the final strategies and goals for your five-part solution:

1. Prerequisite Individual Learning History

A learning history is a document that tells a typical story from a project that is over. The story chosen should illustrate the typical issues the project team had to deal with. The document should be no more than one page typed, and should relate in as much detail as possible the people involved, the decisions made, and the constraints and any other factors that help explain what happened. Learning histories usually reflect both strengths and weaknesses of projects; they are not exclusively negative.

2. Sharing Learning Histories—2-Hour Session

Each person should bring a copy of his or her individual learning history to the meeting and provide enough copies so that everyone will be able to read along. Each person reads his or her story, and others have an opportunity to ask questions.

After a person has read the learning history and there are no more questions, the person reading summarizes with three lessons learned from the story. The facilitator captures these on a flipchart. It is not necessary that each person has unique lessons learned. It is common for overlap to exist.

3. Prerequisite Team Vision—Three Nouns and a Verb

Each person, before the session, writes a vision for the project using exactly three verbs and one noun. It is useful to give them an example so they get the sense of what they are going to do, but it should be an example that is not project related and won't influence their answer. An example might be:

> *The vision of our project is to plant, water, and cut fresh flowers.*

Note that sometimes it is useful to give people a list of verbs and nouns to choose from, but this might limit their contribution and creativity.

4. Sharing Visions, Consensus, and Rules of Engagement—2 Hour Session

Have everyone share their three verbs and one noun vision statements. Break the group into teams of three, preferably mixing up the two old teams. Have each small group create a combined team vision. Bring these together to create a consensus team vision for their project.

Use this vision to create a list of rules of engagement using a brainstorming technique. Have these rules of engagement made into laminated wallet cards.

5. Scenario Planning—2-Hour Session

Define four possible futures using the variables "project on time" and "team collaboration." Brainstorm how a day in the life of each of these futures would look, and then what events would occur to trigger each future. Finally, ask each person individually to share where he or she thinks the project is now, where he or she thinks the project will go if nothing changes, and where he or she wants to go.

The last step is to build an action plan for project success using a brainstorming technique. Complete the action plan with task owners and due dates.

What You Build

Now it is time for you to design the measurable learning objectives for each part of the proposed solution, determine facilitation requirements, and create materials.

Preparing for the Individual Learning History

Learning Objectives. Each participant will learn about his or her perception of the strengths and weaknesses of the last project that he or she worked on.

Required Equipment and Supplies. You must email directions (including a sample of a well done learning history) to all of the participants at least 1 week before the first session. Then, be sure to print a sufficient number of each learning history's results so that each participant may have one in the session. Lastly, send out a follow-up email 24 hours before the session to remind the participants to attend.

Step-by-Step Design.

1. Construct the email notice, and write up a generic example.

2. Send the notice to each of the project team members. Ask each to bring a completed copy of the learning history.

3. Send a reminder 24 hours before the session to remind people of the prework.

4. If people show up without a learning history in hand, ask them to go to a computer and type it up and copy it right then. Let the others go on with the sharing exercise.

When sending out an example of a learning history, make sure the one you use is very brief and be sure to stress that the document should be telling a typical story. It is not meant to be documentation of the project. You should also make sure the participants know that they will be sharing these stories. If the trust level is too low, skip the copies for others, and just let people read their stories to others.

Top Priority

Amazingly, people will write their real feelings and beliefs, even when they know they are going to be shared with others. Writing often liberates people from their armor of silence.

- It is not a problem if people end up rushing to create their story right before the meeting. In fact, they quicker they do it, the more honest it is likely to be.

- Be careful not to give them an example that influences their own response.

Results. People often don't know how they feel until they read what they have written. They will be thinking differently about their project after they've written their learning history—even before you gather the team together.

The First Session—Lessons Learned

Learning Objectives. Each participant will learn about his or her own view of the successes and failures of the last project he or she worked on. The participants will also learn about how the views of other project team members may differ from their own. At the conclusion of this facilitation, each of the project team members will have a shared understanding of what actually happened on the last project.

Required Equipment and Supplies. You will need to provide a flipchart and markers to note lessons that were learned by the participants in their previous project experiences. After the session, send out a follow-up email that summarizes the flipchart notes from the session.

Step-by-Step Design.

1. If they have made them, ask each participant to distribute the copies of his or her personal learning histories, in turn. While others are reading along, each person will read his or her learning history aloud.

2. As people read, ask the people listening to take brief notes that will help them in the discussion to follow.

3. After a person finishes reading, ask for questions of clarification. To keep it conflict free, ask people to phrase their questions using only what and how, for example, "What happened that caused you to think that the customers wanted a new project manager?" Notice how this is very different in tone to "Why did you think the customers wanted a new project manager?" which appears to be more threatening.

4. When there are no more questions, continue with the next reader until everyone has read his or her learning history.

5. After all have read, approach the flipchart paper. Ask people to share the challenges they heard as people read. If people are not participating equally, consider going around the room and asking each person to contribute one challenge.

6. Next, ask the participants to share something that they heard which helped the project and would be considered a success.

7. Finally, ask the participants to share lessons learned from what they have heard. On a fresh sheet of flipchart paper, document the participants' ideas for how to do projects differently to avoid repeating the mistakes they have just heard about. Translate this into an action plan, with people designated to each step as well as due dates.

It is very easy when facilitating this kind of session to "lead the witness." Limit your comments to active listening (". . . Let me see if I've captured this right, you said the customer disliked you from the start?") and content-oriented what and how questions ("What about the timeline did you find worrisome at the beginning?" or "How would the timeline be different for you to be confident that it could be met?").

Carefully control the discussion. If one person accidentally says something that might offend another, be ready to jump in, enforce the ground rules, and get the group back on track. The point of this exercise is to get the team to have a common view of history. Together, then, they are able to build the action plan, creating a co-owned way of moving forward into this project. Do not get involved with this other than to document what they decided.

If the group gets to a standstill and can't seem to come up with anything else, remember to use silence to motivate them to speak what is on their minds.

Top Priority

People are taking great risks by sharing personal emotions and perceptions of how a project went. In some cases, they may be sharing stories about each other. When people are allowed to honestly express themselves in this way, other team members begin to empathize with each other. It is not unusual to hear, "Wow, I never knew you felt that way," and "I had no idea you had invested so much time into that task." Help the team see that:

- Project team members never see the whole project. It is important to bring teams together to see the whole, instead of just the separate parts.

- Everyone carries their own "war wounds" into the next project if no one allows them time to vent and heal.

- Sharing pain with others creates a strong trust in the group.

Results. After this discussion, the team is ready to look forward to the project they are currently on together. Use this increased trust to move into setting up ground rules for the project—a task that most teams avoid tackling.

Preparing for the Individual Team Vision

Learning Objectives. Each participant learns about his or her own vision for the project.

Required Equipment and Supplies. Contact all the participants with a friendly email that contains an example vision statement and instructions on how to create their own. As you did with the first session, 24 hours before the session send out a reminder email in case it slipped anyone's mind.

Step-by-Step Design.

1. Construct the email notice, and write up a generic example. An example might be "On this project, we analyze, code, and implement a sales solution."

2. Send the example to each of the project team members. Ask each to create a vision for the project using three verbs and one noun. Connecting words are OK.

3. Send a reminder 24 hours before the session to remind people of the prework and of the session itself.

4. If people show up without their project vision, ask them to create one quickly before the session starts.

Make the example you create for the email notice very brief. Stress that the vision is their preferred vision, not necessarily the vision of anyone else. If people come late and do not have a vision, they will still be able to help prioritize the others' thoughts. If no one has done the vision, take the time at the beginning of the session to let people silently and alone create one.

Top Priority

People will be honest in how they interpret the goal of the project even if they think it will conflict with the views of others in the group. Writing often liberates people from their armor of silence.

- If people scramble to write their statement at the beginning of the session, that's OK. Often, writing is more honest when it is done quickly.

- Be careful not to give them an example that influences their own response. Stay vague and instead focus on adhering to the sentence construction guidelines.

Results. Many people have never really stopped and thought about what a project is all about. This exercise forces people to be specific about what their role is on the project, and how the project fits into the strategies of the business.

The Second Session—Rules of Engagement and Team Vision

Learning Objectives. Each participant will participate in building a common list of rules of engagement to reinforce good collaborative team behavior owned by the team itself. In addition, the team will come to a consensus on a unified team vision that should create alignment among team members no matter their past projects.

Required Equipment and Supplies. As usual, you should bring a flipchart and markers to make note of rules of engagement and team vision ideas. You will also need Post-it notes, and, as for the first session, you should send out a follow-up email with the summarized flipchart notes to all of the participants.

Step-by-Step Design

1. Rules of engagement: Explain that rules of engagement are the rules that each member of the team will be expected to follow after they are established to make it easier to work together. Ask each participant to take out some Post-it notes. They will be putting one idea on each Post-it note. Give them between 5 and 10 minutes to think of rules that would be appropriate for the following categories that you have written on a flipchart page:

   a. Email Etiquette (reply, CC, appropriate use)
   b. Meeting Manners (lateness, preparation, interruptions)
   c. Presentation Policies (length, purpose, questions, PowerPoint slides)
   d. Phone Facts: (voicemail messages, checking, when to return calls)
   e. Other:

2. As people begin to stack up their ideas in front of them, gather them up, and group them under the category that makes the most sense.

3. After people seem to slow down, read the ideas to the group. Gather more thoughts and ideas if they come up.

4. Break into five teams, and assign each team one of the categories. In 10 to 15 minutes, ask them to create "Rules of Engagement" from the Post-It notes in their category.

5. Have each team read their resulting rules. If possible, have them write them on flipchart paper so that people can review them multiple times. Ask for suggestions on how to improve these rules.

6. After each team's results are discussed, read through the entire list once more. Remind them that you will be emailing this list to them and ask for additional comments. This entire process takes approximately 1 hour.

7. Now onto the team vision exercise. Ask participants to take out the team vision that they created as prerequisite work. If some have not, encourage them to take a few minutes to create three verbs and a noun describing the vision of the project. Have participants write each word (the three verbs and one noun) on an individual Post-it note. Again, collect these and group them together on a flipchart page toward the front of the room.

8. When you have collected all the Post-it notes, read the results to the group. Discuss if any of the verbs or nouns are similar and whether they should be combined.

9. Ask the participants to take out a pencil and explain that each person has 10 votes. They may use their votes any way they want: They can put all 10 votes on one verb that they really feel strongly about or put one vote on 10 different words. They vote by placing a checkmark on the Post-it note containing the word they are voting for.

10. When everyone has voted, summarize the results. Select the top three verbs and one noun and write them on a flipchart page as a draft team vision. Lead a discussion around the meaning of each of the words and whether the words require additional adjectives or adverbs to make the meaning clear.

11. Send a follow-up email containing both the rules of engagement and the team vision.

Again, be sure not to "lead the witness." Limit your comments to active listening statements ("Just to confirm, you said the product timeline was unreasonable?") and content-oriented what and how questions ("What about customer relations did you find worrisome at the beginning?" or "How would the timeline be different if you were in charge?").

You must carefully control the discussion. If one person accidentally says something that might offend another, be ready to jump in, enforce the ground rules, and get the group back to the task at hand.

Force the team to address the measurability and accountability of the rules of engagement. Lead a discussion around the question, "Who will enforce the rules, and how will they be enforced?" Take the team through the difficult conversation the members would probably rather not have.

When working with the verbs and nouns, it is often helpful to have people create one-line descriptions to ensure that everyone is clear what the words mean. For example, how would the team differentiate the verbs "manage" and "lead"?

Top Priority

At this point, the team has been through some deep discussions with each other, building a trust that will be necessary to move into the third session. Help the team celebrate this accomplishment so its members are aware of how differently they are communicating with each other. Emphasize that:

- Sometimes it takes a little structure that may seem like overkill to ensure that teams work well together. Everybody needs something different, and it is important for a team to establish common ground for their interactions.

- The team can use its vision to assign priorities to work and get over trouble spots when members disagree. Help the team focus the vision on the customer, not the team. For example, a team vision that says, "We support, defend, and empower the other team members" is not a project that will add any value to the business.

Results. The team is now ready to move into a hard look at the future of the project. Utilizing the rules of engagement and the team vision in the next session helps ensure that the team continues to move toward project success.

The Third Session—Scenario Planning

Learning Objectives. Now that the participants have agreed on rules of engagement and a team vision, it is time to get more specific. After completing this scenario-planning session, the participants identify how everyday decisions affect progress toward the team vision.

Required Equipment and Supplies. A flipchart and markers are necessary to take note of important statements in the session. As for the first two sessions, you should also send out a follow-up email that summarizes the flipchart notes so that everyone is on the same page.

Step-by-Step Design.
1. Post the team vision on the wall so everyone can refer to it.

2. Post the figure 4-2 on another flipchart page so all can see it.

3. Go over each of the quadrants. Explain that each describes a future state for the current project.

4. The overall process is to have team members first describe "a day in the life" at the end of the project and then describe, working backward, the events that

Figure 4-2. The four-quadrant approach for projects.

QUADRANT 1: Heaven	QUADRANT 2: Unhealthy
On Time Happy Team	On Time Stressed-Out Team
QUADRANT 3: **Out of Business**	**QUADRANT 4:** **The Trash Can**
Late Happy Team	Late Stressed-Out Team

would have to occur to make the project end up like that. This is done for every quadrant.

5. It saves time to split the team in half to work concurrently. If you have enough people to split into four teams, this will work as well. Each smaller group will take 5 minutes to document on flipchart paper what a "day in the life" would look like with the project as their assigned quadrant describes. Post this list of brainstorming ideas to get them started. Consider:

   - What are the stakeholders like?
   - What is the client involvement?
   - What is the budget like?
   - What has happened to the rules of engagement?
   - Has there been turnover or illness?
   - What are the deliverables of the project like?
   - What are some of the roadblocks and success factors?
   - What processes are being followed?
   - What is the organizational structure?

6. Have each team report back to the larger group and tell their stories. Encourage the listeners to check for inconsistency, for example, there is no budget but the manager buys pizza for the team every day. Discuss the stories and add to them if it makes sense. Keep this moving and limit the time to 10 minutes total.

7. Have the groups return to their analysis and list events that would have to happen starting today to make their quadrant, as described by their story, come true for 5 minutes. For example, if the stakeholders are currently very involved, what might happen to cause them to not be involved at all? Give the teams permission to be very creative here. They can think up and add any events that logically would contribute the cause-and-effect situation. The caveat is that the events have to flow together to support the entire scenario as described in the last step. Again, have each team report back to the larger group and share their events. Expect some laughter and some "burns" in this discussion. Again, ask the listeners to verify consistency. Limit the time to 10 minutes.

8. Ask each team member, one at a time, to go up to the table and indicate the following by initialing the poster:

   - where he or she thinks the project is now
   - where he or she thinks the project is going if nothing else changes
   - where he or she wants the project to go.

9. After this candid discussion, spend at least 15 minutes building an action plan. Ask team members to contribute what needs to be done to ensure that the project moves to the quadrant they want it to move toward. This will be the list that you will send out via email as a summary after the session.

Tips. During discussions, limit your own comments to active listening and content-oriented what/how questions, but be ready to control the discussion if one person accidentally says something that might offend another. Enforce the ground rules, and get the group back on track. Be especially aware when people are sharing their own beliefs about the current or future state of the project.

Watch out for lazy thinking. It is possible to do scenario planning without getting into much interesting thought. As teams share the results of their stories, challenge them to take it one more step. For example, if a team says, "Everyone has their résumé out" ask them what other behaviors occur because everyone has their résumé out.

By the time the team gets to action planning, the members may be a bit tired. If necessary, have them brainstorm actions using Post-It notes when a full discussion is not working out. Moving people around can help, too. If the action planning is not going very well because of lack of energy, try asking people to share ways to ensure that the project goes into the "straight into the trash can" quadrant. After a couple of minutes of this, complete with laughter, the team should refocus on the positive.

Top Priority

These three sessions combined will have helped the team begin to see one another as thinking individuals. The first session helped them build trust and a way of clearing out the baggage from previous projects. The second helped them create a common language for behavior and the vision of the project. In this final session, you have forced the team to look honestly at the future of the project and their contribution to either its demise or success. From all three, you have action plans to encourage them to adopt new collaborative behaviors.

To close this engagement, set up some time with the project manager a couple of weeks after the third session. Coach the project manager to use the language of the three sessions and enforce the rules of engagement.

Results. After the third session, the team is ready to return to the project with new thoughts. They will be able to see and talk about decisions and events that might trigger the project's slide into an unhappy scenario.

Measuring Your Success

The goal of the project manager at the beginning of this initiative was to get the team collaborating quickly to save this critical project.

Measuring the success of the project (how close to budget, how close to deadlines) is not really going to tell you if the team is collaborating; too many variables other than team collaboration can affect these numbers. Instead, consider setting up a baseline at the start of this project. Ask each individual team member to rate their "comfort with the team" from 1 to 10, 1 being low. Have them give you these numbers privately (perhaps even through email) and average the results. Repeat this exercise after the final session.

Debrief

In this chapter, you have learned about a pretty typical situation. Usually by the time the training department is called, the team has built a strong habit of not getting along. A common solution is a quick 1-day session, but this approach can actually add to the disagreement and bad feelings because the problem will seem to have been trivialized. Teams do not go bad overnight, so helping them choose to get back on track is not a quick process. Multiple sessions over time are necessary although the sessions do not have to be very long.

As was true in the scenario presented here, help requires more than just team building in the traditional sense. It requires rebuilding the trust the team had destroyed and replacing bad norms with good. The final activity for alignment used scenario planning to build a shared vision. All team interventions require building trust, positive shared behaviors and a shared vision.

The result of fostering collaboration is an aligned, resilient project team. This should greatly contribute to the success of the project, but if the project has other risk factors, improved team functioning may not be enough.

In the next chapter, you will read about a situation where a whole information technology organization has degraded into a large dysfunctional team. A breakdown in trust degrades everything else, and trust is very difficult to re-create.

Activity 4-1. Individual learning history.

1. Reflect on the project that you most recently completed. In this space, jot down any thoughts you have about what frustrated you about this project and what you would do differently were you to repeat it:

2. In the space below, write down what went well on the project, and lessons learned that you would utilize for future projects:

3. Finally, use the space below and the back of this sheet, if needed, to write a story that was typical of the kind of thing that happened on this project. Think about how this story represents the good and the not-so-good aspects of the entire experience. Please limit your writing to approximately three to five paragraphs:

Activity 4-1

Activity 4-2. Rules of engagement.

Think of ground rules that would help your teams work more effectively together.

Consider the following and jot down your ideas:

- Meeting conduct:

- Email conduct:

- Project communication:

- Customer service:

- Phone/voicemail conduct:

- Social conduct (for example, saying hello in the hall, keeping lunch appointments):

- Other:

Activity 4-2

Activity 4-3. Scenario planning example.

QUADRANT 1: Heaven	QUADRANT 2: Unhealthy
On Time Happy Team	On Time Stressed-Out Team
QUADRANT 3: Out of Business	**QUADRANT 4: The Trash Can**
Late Happy Team	Late Stressed-Out Team

Scenario Planning Process:

1. Identify two values that are important to the team.
2. Vary these two values to create four quadrants.
3. Tell the story of how the future could be like the two values in 5 years, creating one story for each quadrant. What would the processes, people, technology, and organization be like? Who would the customers be? What would the product be?
4. For each quadrant, create a list of tasks that would have to occur for the future to occur.
5. Share with the rest of the team where you believe the team is now, where they will be in the future if nothing changes, and where you would like them to be.

Activity 4-3

chapter 5

Technical and Process Training
Spinning the Wheels of Process

A help desk manager has emailed you asking for help with his team. Although his team uses very sophisticated software tools to help communicate issues, the tools aren't used consistently. Instead, each person has his or her own way of working, creating redundant work. Calls are not processed quickly, and big backlogs of work accumulate.

What They Say—The Situation

You: What has happened that triggered this call?

Executive: Our help desk recently did a customer service survey and our results were significantly lower than last year. We're getting worse at customer service, even after investing in some pretty expensive software to streamline our work. I convinced my bosses that this investment would solve some of our response issues, but the opposite has occurred!

You: So, it sounds like you need to improve your customer's perception of your service. What are some of the reasons you think this problem has gotten worse?

Executive: Well, the software should have worked, so the obvious place to start is checking to see if people are using the software the way it was designed. I've done a little digging on this. These are very intelligent people, and my reports seem to indicate that problems and solutions are being logged correctly, but the resolution of the problems is taking longer than it used to. I have noticed that there are often multiple people logging the same problem, which would add to our workload. It seems that we might have some problems with who owns the issues, handoffs, and general communication of what has been done so far with issues. I wouldn't be able to see this kind of breakdown on a report.

You: So, you are getting the reports you need after the fact. It sounds like people updated their software but are using out-of-date communication techniques. What have you noticed that would indicate that this is the case?

Executive: I guess I mistakenly thought that the software would enforce the process, but there are many gaps in the process outside of the software. These gaps must have been the primary issue all along, so the software hasn't helped and, in fact, has added work. If we could fix those gaps, the software could really facilitate quick resolution and accurate tracking, but with the gaps, the software can't create the return I had hoped for.

What You Hear

Your conversation with the client and your research has brought you to the conclusions outlined in table 5-1.

Based on these inferences, you build agreement with the manager that the goals of this process improvement program are the following:

- Improve customer service by streamlining the communication of the help desk staff.

- Improve customer service by reducing rework and redundancy among the help desk.

Table 5-1. Logical conclusions.

What the Client Says	What You Hear
My people need software training.	The new software must be the problem. People aren't using it right even though they don't report any problems with it. Help me figure out what else I can do!
My customers are less happy with our services than they were last year.	Customer feedback is the most important metric to me. No matter what they are upset about, we need to fix it.
My people are solving the problems, but in an inefficient way.	My people are good at what they do and they are dedicated to our customers, but they may be working so independently that work is done twice when handoffs occur. We need to trust each other a bit more perhaps.

- Increase speed of issue resolution at the help desk.

- Because the help desk cannot close, there will be two groups going through the sessions. One group will cover the help desk while the other goes to the session.

What You Do

Begin where all good performance solutions begin—with asking the right questions. Your training and performance instincts have already given you some good guidance, but as is the case with all successful interventions, you first must figure out what's really behind what is said. Here are some questions that you need to ask before the solution can be proposed:

- What types of behavioral changes would you like to see after the program is completed? How would a help desk staff member provide better service to the customer?

- How are problems escalated currently? Who owns the problem after a handoff? Who follows up with the customer to ensure that the customer's needs have been met?

- When is the software used during the process? How do handoffs occur through the software?

- What is a reasonable goal for customer service results for next year? How long would it take after changes to see this change?

- What is a reasonable goal for average time to solve a customer problem? How long would it take after changes to see this change?

Results of Questions

You have learned from asking these questions that:

- There are three levels of escalation: Tier 1 (answers the phone, basic knowledge base through the software), Tier 2 (more advanced general knowledge), and Tier 3 (SME).

- The last handoff currently is perceived to own the problem. However, each level believes it is responsible for issue logging, generating double or triple records related to the same problem.

- Tier 3 SMEs are highly technical. Tier 1 staff have the strongest people skills. Follow-up will be done by Tier 1 after a problem is solved, so this group will retain ownership even after escalation.

- Within 6 months, the help desk manager would like to see an improvement of 25 percent in customer service (as measured by the customer service survey) and a decrease of 15 percent in the time required to solve a problem (as measured by the reports from the software).

Your Triage Intervention

Upon consulting with the executive, you have identified several constraints around which this learning intervention must function. First, there are 16 people staffing the help desk. The sessions must be short (less than half a day) to ensure that half of the staff can be covering for the other while they are learning. The manager, however, will attend all of the sessions. Second, the sessions must begin in 2 weeks and be completed 2 weeks after the starting time.

You have proposed to the manager the plan shown in figure 5-1, and he has accepted.

Session 1 (3 hours):

- Four Facts, a quick team-building exercise. **Purpose:** Increase the trust between staff and help desk staff as people get to know each other outside the work environment.

- Signatures Simulation. **Purpose:** Amplify the very problems that are challenging the help desk.

- Metaphor Sculptures for the help desk staff. **Purpose:** Develop a team vision of the help desk and create artifacts to leave in the office to reinforce the lessons learned from the sessions. Sculptures will also serve to connect the separate groups.

Figure 5-1. Your technical and training process intervention.

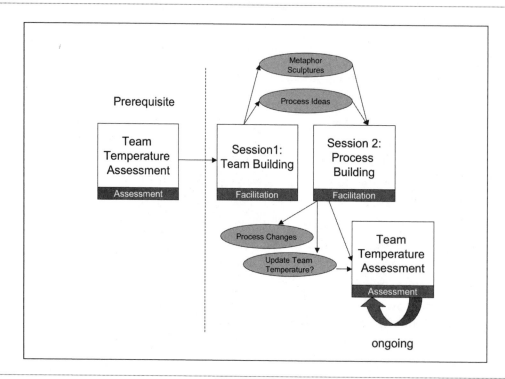

Session 2 (3 hours):

- Handoff and Communication Process Design Dialogue. **Purpose:** Create common processes specifying owners, steps, handoff points, communication points, and measures.

- Team Temperature Assessment. **Purpose:** Create a set of five to 10 assessment criteria to use 6 months after the session to check the perceived trust and communication success of the help desk staff.

- Magic of 9's. **Purpose:** Reinforce the importance of internal communication during handoffs as a closing activity.

You only have 2 weeks to build the initial executive session, then 2 weeks after that to complete all four sessions. The solution is broken down into more detailed overviews in the following sections.

Prerequisite: Team Temperature Assessment

This prerequisite assessment (activity 5-1) will be used so that the participants will start with a shared view of the problem. This prerequisite will contain questions written by you, the consultant; but in session 2, the help desk staff will build new questions to use for checking the team temperature on an ongoing basis. Web-based assessments would be simpler to do than paper-based instruments, and the data would be easier to summarize.

Session 1: Four Facts, Signatures, and Metaphor Sculptures

In this session, the help desk staff (split into two different classes) will begin to identify the communication problems they have and start to grow a shared vision of what the communication should be like.

Opening with the Four Facts activity will help each person appreciate the diversity of his or her co-workers. It is not uncommon for people who have worked together to think they know everything about each other. This type of exercise usually proves that mentality wrong.

The Signatures Simulation can provoke similar communication patterns to the ones causing problems in the team presently. You, as facilitator, will be able to debrief extensively on these problems and help the participants see what the communication issues are.

Finally, breaking into small teams and creating Metaphor Sculptures gets them to discuss the essentials of good communication. You will facilitate a brief discussion of the characteristics of communication that these metaphors represent. The Metaphor Sculptures from each team will be exchanged at the beginning of session 2.

Session 2: Handoff and Communication Dialogue, Team Temperature Assessment, Magic of 9's

At the beginning of the second session, participants will view the Metaphor Sculptures from the other group, and you will facilitate a brief discussion of the characteristics of communication that these metaphors represent (similar to the first session).

At this point, you have reinstated the trust that was initially built in the first session. The teams are ready to discuss common communication scenarios and build a model for handoffs and communication.

The group will then build a list of suggested questions for the ongoing Team Temperature Assessment and end with a quick closing activity using the Magic of 9's to reinforce that, although they bring many diverse strengths to the help desk, they are all similar in their need for communication and their need to help their internal customers.

Ongoing Team Temperature Assessment

You will review the proposed questions from both of the sessions, and create a new Team Temperature Assessment to be used every 6 months.

What You Build

The plan is approved, and now it is time for you to design the measurable learning objectives for each part of the proposed solution, determine facilitation requirements, and create materials. At this time, you must also establish appropriate learning objectives. In this case, each participant will learn how the entire team views the communication problems.

Prerequisite Team Temperature Assessment

Required Equipment and Supplies. Assemble the following items prior to undertaking the assessment:

- paper forms or a Web-based assessment (activity 5-1)
- email notification
- tracked email reports to make sure assessments are done on time
- printed results reports (also electronic).

You may use a Web application such as www.surveymonkey.com or even do the surveys using email or paper. The choice depends on your budget and the number of survey participants. As is true for any survey, the more responses, the better the results. It is critical to ensure that the results will remain completely anonymous and that the language is very clear. Consider testing the initial questions on a few help desk staff members before rolling it out to everyone.

Step-by-Step Design.

1. Determine from the executive sponsor the type of communication problems that are rumored to be occurring. Create questions that do not "lead the witness" and allow the person to respond that an item is "not applicable."

2. Force the person to take a stand by using an even number of responses, such as a rating scale from 1 to 4, to eliminate the middle-of-the-road response of 3 on a scale from 1 to 5. This is shown in the example assessment provided as activity 5-1.

3. Send the survey to all the members with a clear "return by" date, or else do the assessments quickly during other face-to-face meetings to get a better return.

4. Create material to distribute in the first session to summarize the responses.

Tips. Create questions that address how a learner views the communication practiced by those around him or her and the communication exercised by him- or herself. That way you can see whether people as a whole see the problem as their own, everybody else's, or a mixture. Also be sure to limit the questions to no more than 10. People stop thinking when assessments involve more than 10 items.

Survey Results. For illustration, assume that the results show that the vast majority of the staff believe there is a communication problem. They feel overwhelmingly that the team avoids difficult conversations and holds communication with others as a low priority. The interesting conflict is that most individuals do not believe that they personally have a problem with communication. This disconnect will be useful when you begin session 1 and share these results.

Session 1: Four Facts

To open the first session, you ask each participant to write down four facts about him- or herself, one of which is false. The others will try to guess which fact is not true.

Learning Objectives. After participating in Four Facts, each learner will

- question their own personal labels for others
- broaden their appreciation of the complexity of others
- see others as whole, interesting people
- begin to enjoy each other's company (laugh!).

Required Equipment and Supplies. All you need for Four Facts is scrap paper and pencils for writing.

Step-by-Step. Here are the steps for foolproof implementation of Four Facts:

1. Make sure each participant has blank paper and a writing implement.

2. Explain that all the participants will write down four facts about themselves that they will read to the others. Explain that one (and only one) of these facts will be a lie. Write your Four Facts on a flipchart paper as an example, but do not tell them what your lie is yet. For example:

   I enjoy camping.
   I was captain of the lacrosse team in high school.
   I got my first computer last year.
   I have published a book.

3. When you are done writing your Four Facts, give the participants time to write down their facts.

4. Return to your example. Read your four facts and ask people to vote on which one is the lie. Tell them. Now, break into teams of three to help move this exercise along or else it can take forever. Have each team do exactly what you did: Each person will share with the other two and then identify the lie when voting is done. Then have each team select the best Four Facts set in their group to share with everyone.

5. Each of the winners will share their Four Facts with the group. When this is done, debrief briefly by asking anyone what surprised him or her the most about what was heard. Help people discover that people tend to assume things about those with whom they work, but these assumptions aren't always accurate.

Tips. To make this activity a meaningful part of your triage intervention, be sure to do the following:

- Encourage people to share surprising truths in their Four Facts, but keep them appropriate to work (of course).

- Keep this exercise moving along; it is not difficult for it to drag or for discussion to take a side track because of the interesting facts coming up.

- Be sure to close with debriefing to bring the exercise back to task. This opening activity might seem disconnected to anything of consequence to people who aren't sure they want to be at the session at all.

- Be careful to control the debriefing. If someone says "I am so surprised that Bill is a Sunday school teacher because I've never heard him say a civil word!" be quick to respond. I like to bring out Negasaurus whenever someone starts to sound negative, trigger the toy dinosaur's roar, and give him to the offender saying "Oh! That's negative, so you get Negasaurus! It's your job to catch the next person being negative." This will get everyone laughing, and give you a powerful way to keep the discussion from hurting people.

Top Priority

When debriefing the group, use these questions:

- Which true fact surprised you the most? Why?

- Which false facts threw you off the most? Why?

- What have you learned about how well you know each other?

- What assumptions have you made that might be hindering your ability to communicate with each other? (If this question is too tough, have them write their responses on their own and not share.)

Session 1: Signatures Simulation

In this quick, simple simulation, you will catch people behaving in ways that hinder communication similarly to the problems in their current team. You may find that people:

■ tend to tell rather than ask when they are in a team situation

■ compete with each other rather than work collaboratively

■ resist asking for clarification when something is not clear

■ react quickly instead of thinking about what they are trying to accomplish.

Learning Objectives. After completing this simulation, the participants will be able to:

■ identify some communication problems that exist in the team

■ recognize beliefs and assumptions that trigger these problems.

Required Equipment and Supplies. Assemble the following items prior to undertaking Signatures Simulation:

■ flipcharts and markers

■ scrap paper and pencils for writing

■ a timer, watch, or clock.

■ a requirements sheet as a handout, one per team of three (provided as activity 5-2).

Step-by-Step. If you follow these ordered steps, you should be able to run a successful Signatures Simulation:

1. Break the room into teams of three to four participants, and tell the groups that the person who was born farthest from the room we're in will play the role of the leader. (Pets can be a tie breaker, if need be.) The leaders are the ultimate authority, and they do not have to do anything to help if they don't want to.

2. Give each team a requirements sheet. Tell them they have 2 minutes to create a strategy. They can't begin until you tell them to.

3. After 2 minutes, tell everyone they have 3 minutes to complete this assignment. Tell them to begin. Start your timer.

4. Observe the behaviors of the teams, making notes to use during the debrief. Try to stay low key and keep away. Don't call attention to yourself.

5. Give the teams a warning after each minute. Tell groups to stop after 3 minutes and return to their tables to count their results. Ask the teams to share the number of signatures they acquired by saying "Which team thinks it is the winner? How many did you get?" This language will continue to encourage win-lose behavior.

6. Give a prize to the team with the most signatures. (No need to count or verify the numbers.) There might be some grumbling from people who didn't win. Begin the debriefing by asking: "Does anyone want to challenge the results?" At this point, another team may complain that the winning team cheated. Continue the debriefing.

Tips. Resist the temptation to say more than necessary. The fewer instructions the better because you are trying to catch people in suboptimal communication behaviors. Act as if you have given them all the information they need.

If one of the teams approaches you with a question about the requirements, answer them quietly so that other teams don't notice. If a team asks you if the signatures have to be unique, quietly tell them no. If a team asks you if they can sign their own signature over and over again, or if they can leave the room, quietly tell them yes. It is likely no one will ask you any of these things because most people will assume answers and continue with their strategy without asking.

Top Priority

Debrief using the following process and write key ideas on a flipchart:

- Ask the winning team what they did to make them successful. When you've captured that team's thoughts, ask other teams what they did that made them successful. You should elicit such responses as:

  — We worked well together as a team.

  — We communicated well as a team.

  — We had a really creative idea.

  — We had a very clear, shared goal.

- Ask all the teams what they would do differently next time. Listen for:

  — We would be more flexible and change our strategy if it wasn't working.

  — We would spend more time strategizing to get a more creative strategy.

  — We would learn from others and adapt.

  — We would take the time to ask for clarification.

Continue debriefing using some of these questions:

- What prevented you from asking me for clarification? I like to really pester teams at this point because they rarely ask any questions and seem to prefer to assume answers. Some of their reasons have been:

  — If we asked you, you would have told us we can't do it. (Is it better to do it fast and wrong, rather than slow and right?)

  — We didn't know we could ask questions (assumptions about communication).

  — It's more fun to do it the way we wanted to (lack of alignment with the team or customer).

- What effect do the pressures to be fast have on communication?

- What effect does competition among teams have on communication?

- What prevented teams from collaborating on this project?

The results of this exercise set the stage for finishing up Session 1 by building Metaphor Sculptures.

Session 1: Metaphor Sculptures

This is an individual exercise. Each person will represent a metaphor by making a sculpture of modeling clay. The metaphor should symbolize how they wish communication would be within the help desk team.

Learning Objectives. After completing their Metaphor Sculpture, the participant will

- describe how he or she would like the help desk communication to change
- list the competencies making up good communication within the help desk team.

Required Equipment and Supplies. Before beginning this activity, assemble the following items:

- Modeling clay or Playdough modeling compound (three colors per person). The small party-favor packs work best.
- A small plastic plate to put the structure on so it can be transported to the next session.
- A small index card to list the competencies of communication.

Step-by-Step. Playing with modeling compound is one of the things that brings most people back to the lightness of playing as a child. Thinking of metaphors does not come easily for many adults. The business world does not usually have the time to think creatively like this. Sculpting helps people loosen up their brains. Many will be reluctant initially, but once they get started, they will be fine.

1. Pass out the modeling clay or compound, plates, and index cards.

2. Explain that each person will create a sculpture representing a metaphor for how he or she would like communication to occur within the help desk. Explain that you will help them figure out how to proceed in small steps.

   — Have everyone list three competencies that would lead to great communication on their index card.

   — Looking at these competencies, have people think of something that represents them.

   — Once they think of a metaphor, they are ready to build it. Encourage them to share if they need additional colors.

3. After all the participants have completed their sculptures, ask people one at a time to bring them to the front of the room and explain the metaphor and competencies. Document on the flipchart a list of unique competencies. (There will probably be many that are repeated on multiple sculptures.)

4. Summarize the list and close by asking people to think about processes that could be put in place to encourage these competencies by the next session. Share with the group how this might happen:

   — I wrote down on my index card "trust," "listening," and "honesty."

— I thought about metaphors that fit these three words, and I came up with the metaphor of a baby. After all, babies trust everyone, listen constantly, and can't be anything but honest.

— I built a little baby basket and baby out of clay.

Tips. If someone gets stuck on this activity, go to that person and help him or her with the thought process. Be careful not to "lead the witness," though. Instead, ask the person questions that move him or her through self-discovery.

As you might have guessed, some of these sculptures will be very good and some will not. The sculpture is not as important as the thinking and reflecting, so focus on that.

Session 2: Sharing Metaphor Sculptures

This will be a brief opening to return teams to how they felt after the last session and connect the two teams to each other.

Learning Objectives. After completing the sculpture sharing, the participants will be able to:

- recall and describe how they would like the help desk communication to change
- add to the list the competencies of good communication within the help desk
- collaborate with the participants from the other session.

Required Equipment and Supplies. All you need to complete this activity are the sculptures from both groups that attended session 1.

Step-by-Step.

1. As participants enter, ask them to review the sculptures displayed on a large table. To begin session 2:

   a) Ask each person to write down the one competency he or she thinks is most critical to improving the communication within the help desk staff.

   b) Ask each person to pair up with one other person, and share the most critical competency chosen. Ask the pair to come up with one competency between them that is most critical to improving communication.

   c) Ask each pair to pair up again with another pair. Repeat the process in step a.

   d) Capture on flipchart paper the competencies for each group of four.

Tips.

- This is meant to be a very brief opening exercise. Do not give people very much time to pair up, share, and make choices.
- It is not so critical what competencies make the list, but rather that the participants have revisited the competencies thought about in session 1.

Recall that the help desk staff had to divide into two groups in order to maintain coverage during the sessions.

Session 2: Handoff and Communication Process

This will be a team exercise. Two teams will each create their own process, and then the two teams will combine to create a common process.

Learning Objectives. After completing the process construction, the teams will be able to identify how the scenarios that occur during normal help desk communication can be improved and validate these processes using the competencies established in the opening exercise.

Required Equipment and Supplies. You will need the following items for this activity:

- construction paper (multiple colors)
- yarn
- masking tape
- colored markers that will not bleed through paper onto walls
- large wall areas.

Step-by-Step. Here are the steps for this follow-up activity:

1. Lead a discussion around the typical scenarios for communication within the help desk. Make a list of at least five of these scenarios on a piece of flipchart paper. Use activity 5-3 as a handout.

2. Pile the construction paper, markers, yarn, and tape in a central area. Divide the participants in half, and assign each team to a large wall area.

3. Using the construction supplies provided, ask each team to start with any scenario and build a process that creates good communication and good results for that scenario. Each piece of construction paper will indicate a step in the process. Each step should have the name of an "owner" written on it specifying who is responsible this step. Construction paper can also be used to show results or information that will be handed off to other steps and people. The yarn will be used to show how the steps flow together. See figure 5-2 to see how this works.

4. After the teams have completed a process, ask them to move to another scenario and see if their process still works. At this point they are trying to build a generic process for communication that works in most scenarios. Ask them to modify their process to meet this goal.

5. After the generic process is built, share the two processes with the whole group. Lead a discussion using the questions listed in the "Top Priority" section to clarify how the handoffs and communication are critical to the success of the process. If there is time, combine into one process.

Figure 5-2. Example of the handoff and communication activity.

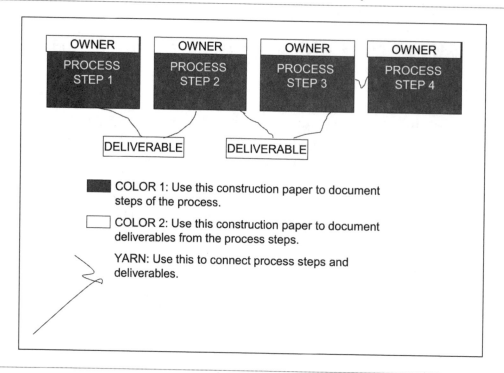

Tips. Keep these ideas in mind:

■ Building tactile processes helps people physically understand how they occur.

■ It is easier to save these construction projects if you build them on blank flipchart paper taped to the wall.

Top Priority

Debrief using the following process and capture ideas on a flipchart for all to see:

■ How does your new process differ from the way communication occurs now? Tell a story of how the old way works, and then retell the story with how the new process would flow.

■ Where are the handoffs in this process? How can you minimize the handoffs?

■ Who owns each of the steps of the process?

■ How would you know, if you were the owner of one of these steps, that the step was completed? How would completion be measured?

Session 2: Team Temperature Assessment Update

This will be an individual exercise. Each individual will brainstorm questions on index cards to add to the Team Temperature Assessment used for ongoing measurement.

Learning Objectives. After completing these new questions, the participant will have a complete understanding of the Team Temperature Assessment.

Required Equipment and Supplies. For this activity, all you need to provide are Post-It notes and pencils.

Step-by-Step.

1. Pass out the pads of Post-It notes and pencils.

2. Display the statements in the original Team Temperature Assessment (activity 5-1).

3. Ask each person to write a question or statement on a Post-It note that they would like to add to the Team Temperature Assessment or modify a question that is already on the assessment.

4. Divide the participants into four groups and assign each group to a wall it is close to. Ask each participant to silently put his or her Post-It note on the near wall.

5. Once all the Post-It notes have been placed on a wall, ask participants to silently group similar Post-It notes together. Have them do this for about 3 minutes.

6. Using a new Post-It note, ask each group to create a question that represents each grouping.

7. Share these questions with the entire group. You, as facilitator, will capture these to update the Team Temperature Assessment after the session.

Session 2: The Magic of 9's

This is a brief closing activity to emphasize how similar people are.

Learning Objectives. After completing these new questions, the participant will view others as similar to him- or herself.

Step-by-Step. These are the essential steps for the Magic of 9's activity:

1. Ask people to pick a number between 2 and 10. Make sure they know not to tell you what it is.

2. Ask people to multiply their number by 9.

3. Ask people to take the two-digit number they have now and add the two digits together.

4. Ask people to subtract 5 from their number.

5. Now, by relating their number to the alphabet, ask them to come up with a country that starts with the letter corresponding to their number (for example, A = 1, B = 2, C = 3, D = 4, E = 5, and so forth). Note that if they have done the math right, the number will always be four, and the letter will be D.

6. Ask people to think of a country that starts with that letter. (Most will think of Denmark.)

7. Ask people to think of an animal that starts with the *second letter* of the country they thought of. (Most will think of an elephant.)

8. Ask people to think of the color of the animal as they picture and imagine it in their heads as you pretend to read their minds. (Most will picture their elephant as gray.)

9. Announce "How many people have thought of a gray elephant from Denmark?"

Tips. Here are a few suggestions to make this activity run smoothly:

■ Work with a group of exemplary communicators and get their help building the initial team temperature assessment and the common scenarios.

■ If there is no time or buy-in to do the assessment as prework, do it in class. Summarize it over the first break and share at that time.

■ Consider mixing up the participants so the roster for session 1 is different than session 2.

■ If people miss session 1 but want to participate in session 2, ask them to build a Metaphor Sculpture as a prerequisite.

■ Encourage the sponsor of this effort to formalize the process created from session 2. Documenting this process and reinforcing the behavior through compliance documents, job descriptions, and performance reviews will increase the odds of lasting change.

Measuring Your Success

The Team Temperature Assessment is designed to provide ongoing feedback and measurement for the team. These results should be communicated and discussed widely each time. In addition, approximately once a year, staff members should reevaluate the appropriateness of the questions.

Debrief

"Why doesn't the help desk help?" is a refrain that is heard often. I'm not sure I ever heard someone say, "Wow, that help desk person was great and really helped me," and certainly no one ever communicates that sentiment to the help desk person. It's a thankless job staffed by people who really like the challenge of solving problems under pressure. But, they can't do that job unless other people in the organization help them in many ways.

Notice how this intervention also contains a process (and assessment) to monitor both the improvement and the degradation of service. Many companies invest in initiatives to solve a problem, but few consider investing in the long-term maintenance of the solution.

In the next chapter you'll read about what can happen when sales staff are under tremendous pressure in the face of change. Sales are up, but so are the numbers of unhappy customers and burned-out salespeople. Your client thinks that a stress management session is the answer, but is it?

Activity 5-1. Team temperature assessment.

Rate the following statements about the communication within your product teams from 1 = completely false to 6 = completely true:

1. The help desk supports me so I can be more productive.	1 2 3 4 5 6
2. The help desk staff are professional and helpful.	1 2 3 4 5 6
3. The help desk staff follow up to make sure my problem is OK.	1 2 3 4 5 6
4. The help desk answers my questions quickly.	1 2 3 4 5 6
5. The help desk is available when I need it.	1 2 3 4 5 6
6. The help desk staff treat me with respect.	1 2 3 4 5 6
7. The help desk staff understand my business needs.	1 2 3 4 5 6
8. The help desk function is critical to our business.	1 2 3 4 5 6
9. Many individuals are unfriendly and want to be alone.	1 2 3 4 5 6
10. Many individuals are perfectionists at the expense of the project.	1 2 3 4 5 6
11. Many individuals are politically motivated and want to look good.	1 2 3 4 5 6
12. Many individuals are moving too fast and ignoring quality.	1 2 3 4 5 6
13. The leadership encourages interteam competition and mistrust.	1 2 3 4 5 6
14. Our current project goals are not possible.	1 2 3 4 5 6
15. Blaming others is very common when we have trouble on projects.	1 2 3 4 5 6

Activity 5-1

Activity 5-2. Project requirements handout.

Goal:

To get as many signatures as possible in 2 minutes.

Process:

1. Spend 3 minutes of strategizing, then bid on how many signatures your team will get, and then take 2 minutes to implement.
2. Get into teams of three to five people.
3. The leader is the person born farthest from this room.

Activity 5-2

Activity 5-3. Sample scenarios.

Help Desk Handoffs:

- VOICEMAIL: The customer left a message.
- VOICEMAIL: Another Help Desk staff member left a voicemail.
- EMAIL: The customer left an email.
- EMAIL: Another Help Desk Staff member left an email.
- ESCALATION: Tier 1 to Tier 2
- ESCALATION: Tier 2 to Tier 3
- ESCALATION: Tier 1 to Tier 3
- PHONE CALL
- EXECUTIVE REQUEST

Activity 5-3

chapter 6

Time Management

There Are Not Enough Hours in a Day!

You have been invited by the vice president of sales to teach a half-day session about managing stress at an internal annual meeting for the salespeople.

What They Say—The Situation

You: What has happened that triggered this call?

Executive: Well, the good news is that our sales are way up. The bad news is that we've had some issues this year. About 10 percent of our salespeople have been fired for submitting overstated numbers and faked orders. This stuff was reported in the newspaper, so we have two things putting pressure on our existing sales staff: concerned customers and fewer salespeople. The sales staff are selling pretty well and our sales are up, but I can tell the people are starting to get really burned out. It's going to be another 6 months before we're able to get additional sales staff, so I'm hoping you can help me figure out how to help the staff we have.

You: So, it sounds like they are still selling, even though the salespeople might be feeling more pressure. Have you notice any other problems from this stress?

Executive: Yes, about 5 percent of our sales staff has left for other jobs, and this number is growing. That just puts more pressure on the salespeople still here. In addition, we are getting a lot more complaints from the installers and the customers that the orders were not what they wanted or were incomplete.

You: So, the salespeople are considering leaving and because of their stress might not be listening as well to the customers or attending to detail like they should. Is that what you've seen?

Executive: Yes, that's it! I'm worried that it's only a matter of time before our sales are affected. With all the negative attention in the press, the last thing we need is a noticeable drop in sales.

What You Hear

Your conversation with the client and your research has brought you to the conclusions listed in table 6-1.

Table 6-1. Logical conclusions.

What the Client Says	What You Hear
Our sales are great, but our sales staff are in a mess.	This is a critical *tipping point*. There's evidence that if something isn't done quickly, the sales and retention will drop.
The salespeople have a right to be burned out. They have little help, but have to keep selling even under challenging circumstances.	Perception is reality. It's possible that the sales staff are assuming that the customers will be hesitant but that the customers aren't really paying attention to the negative press.
There will not be any additional staff to help for 6 months.	The sales staff must learn to prioritize their efforts. They must learn to use their time and efforts more expeditiously.

You build agreement with the executive that there are two goals to this initiative. First, the current growth in sales must be maintained by working with the sales staff to define and help them self-diagnose their current attitudes and beliefs. Second, by teaching the salespeople ways to manage their burnout and stress, the training should reduce and avoid turnover among sales staff. The salespeople and their managers will all partake in this training intervention.

What You Do

Begin where all good performance solutions begin—with asking the right questions. Your training and performance instincts have already given you some good guidance, but as is true for all successful interventions, you first have to figure out what's really behind what is said. Here are some questions that need to be asked before the solution can be proposed:

- What is creating the situation that the sales staff cannot be replaced for 6 months?

- What are the behaviors and symptoms that point to staff burnout?

- How many customers have stopped doing business with the company?

- What is the seniority of the sales staff?

- What was the retention rate before the firings began?

Results of Questions

In this example, you have learned from asking these questions that:

- The sales managers will best be able to describe the changes in behavior that they have seen. They will also be able to share exit interview information about the staff that have taken other jobs.

- There are customers who have been very loyal and who would be willing to talk with you about the current state of the business.

- The salespeople are on full commission, so they are always quite motivated to sell. On a whole, they love to compete with each other.

- The company has been pretty secretive about the problems with the staff who were terminated because of looming litigation. The sales staff has never really been told what happened, and rumors are rampant.

Your Triage Intervention

The executive has presented you two constraints within which your intervention must function. First, the salespeople have an annual sales meeting planned in a month. You will have 1 day to work with them at the conference. The second constraint is that the interviews with the sales managers and customers will have to be completed in the next 2 weeks to meet the deadline for the conference. Keeping these constraints in mind, you have proposed to the executive the plan laid out in figure 6-1, and she has accepted.

- Prerequisite 1-hour individual customer interviews (activity 6-1) and half-day interviews with the sales managers (activity 6-2). **Purpose:** Learn about the customers' perspective and establish behavioral evidence.

- A 1-day workshop at the sales conference including a mini-assessment (activity 6-3), interactions for managing transitions (activities 6-4 and 6-5), managing stress (activity 6-6), setting priorities (activities 6-7 and 6-8), and dealing with burnout (activity 6-9). **Purpose:** Help people become consciously aware of how they are feeling and provide techniques to help them continue to self-diagnose and adjust.

You only have 4 weeks to build the initial executive session, then 4 weeks after that to roll out the initial class for the first participants. More details about the solution are outlined in the following sections.

1. Prerequisite Interviews With the Customers and Sales Managers

To be able to share data with the participants at the start of the 1-day workshop, you have decided to interview key sales managers and key customers. You are going to

Figure 6-1. Your time management intervention.

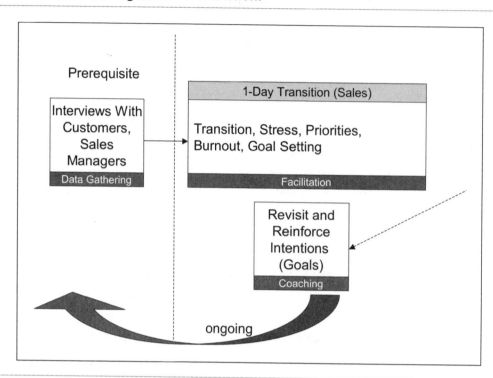

meet with the sales managers together for a half-day group interview, and you are going to talk with the customers over the phone one-on-one for up to an hour.

Starting with the customer allows you to share the data with the sales managers during your interviews with them. When interviewing the customer, you must be careful not to lead the customer into believing things are worse than they are. Good questions to ask during the interview are presented in activity 6-1. Collect this data based on customer responses, and summarize it into brief reports that you will share with the entire group.

When you meet with the sales managers, use the questions in activity 6-2 to guide your discussion. You can also ask the same questions you asked during your requirements gathering. Collect this data and summarize it on flipcharts. Ask the sales managers to prepare a presentation for the sales staff at the next meeting around the lessons they've learned by discussing these questions.

2. 1-Day Workshop at the Sales Convention

As people come into the session, ask them to fill out a mini-assessment (activity 6-3) that consists of just two questions:

- How good is our service to our customers?
- How satisfied are you with your job?

Each response is evaluated on a scale from 1 to 10, one being the lowest. Quickly ask someone to summarize these responses so you can share the results during the session. Then, as an opener, ask the sponsor to introduce you and set the stage for managing transitions. After you are introduced, welcome everyone and ask them to do the first transitions activity.

Transitions: Four Quadrants. This quick, energizing exercise (activity 6-4) will help people see that their own expectations cause at least part of the stress in their jobs.

Transitions: Bridges' Worksheet. This reflective activity (activity 6-5) leads people through the William Bridges' transition model. They will be asked to figure out where they are in their current transition. They will share their results and build a model to depict where they are as an organization.

Managing Stress: Worksheet. The brief worksheet (activity 6-6) will help people see where their own stress is coming from. This will not be shared, unless they opt to release the information.

Managing Stress: Determining Priorities. The reflective exercises for activity 6-7 can help participants figure out what is really important in their lives.

Managing Stress: Pie Chart. Activity 6-8 can help people focus on what is important to them by breaking their day down into time segments to see if the time spent aligns with their priorities.

Dealing With Burnout: Intentions Worksheet. Activity 6-9 is an individual reflective activity. Given the priorities established in the pie chart worksheet, each person writes intentions or goals for where he or she wants to be.

What You Build

The plan is approved, and now it is time for you to design the measurable learning objectives for each part of the proposed solution, determine facilitation requirements, and create course materials.

Prerequisite Interviews With the Customers and Sales Managers

To be able to share data with the participants at the start of the 1-day workshop, you have decided to interview key sales managers and key customers. You are going to meet with the sales managers together for a half-day group interview, and you are going to talk with the customers over the phone one-on-one for up to 1 hour. You use activities 6-1 and 6-2 as sources of questions.

Learning Objectives. The purpose of these interviews is to gather data about how the sales staff is performing from their bosses (sales managers) and their customers.

Required Equipment and Supplies. All you need for this phase in the initiative is note paper for your notes on the phone with the customers and flipchart paper for the session with the sales managers.

Step-by-Step. Follow these steps to implement this activity:

1. Start with the customer (allowing you to share this data with the sales managers later). When interviewing the customer, you must be careful not to lead the customer to believe things are bad if he or she doesn't already. Use the questions in the interview sample provided as activity 6-1.

2. Collect the customer response data and summarize it in brief reports that you share with the entire group.

3. When you meet with the sales managers, begin a discussion around the interview questions in activity 6-2, which includes questions you asked during your requirements gathering.

4. Collect this data and summarize it on flipcharts. Ask the sales managers to prepare a presentation for the sales staff at the next meeting around the lessons they've learned by discussing these questions.

One-Day Workshop

Learning Objectives. After completing the 1-day session, participants will be able to do the following:

- Define the current state of customer service through data from customers and sales managers in the same way.
- Clarify where they are on the managing transitions model based on the work of William Bridges.
- Identify what is important to them and spend their time accordingly.
- Set goals for improving the future and lessening their feelings of burnout.

Required Equipment and Supplies. Prior to the workshop, assemble the following items:

- initial mini-assessment (activity 6-3)
- flipchart paper and markers
- blank paper for activities.

Step-by-Step.

1. As people come into the session, ask them to fill out the mini-assessment. Have someone to summarize these results quickly so you can share the results during the open session.

2. To open the session, ask the sponsor to introduce you and set the stage for managing transitions. After you are introduced, welcome all the participants and ask them to do this first activity.

Transitions: Four Quadrants. Pass out the four-quadrant worksheet (activity 6-4). Make sure everyone has something to write with. Begin by giving them 30 seconds to draw the first time in quadrant 1. Continue giving people 30 seconds to draw the other quadrants with these restrictions:

- Quadrant 2: Draw with your nondominant hand.
- Quadrant 3: Draw with your dominant hand, but with eyes closed.
- Quadrant 4: Draw with your nondominant hand with eyes closed.

As the exercise progresses, you will notice the participants' behavior changing. In the beginning, participants will keep to themselves, quietly and seriously drawing, not sharing at all. By quadrant 4, this will have become a very social activity with participants laughing at themselves and sharing their drawings.

Debrief by pointing out how their behavior changed and asking them why that happened? You want them to self-discover that when people apply the words "should" and "could" to themselves (for example, "I *should* be able to draw"), they add to their own stress. In the last quadrant, people collaborated because they had no expectations of how their drawings would turn out.

At this time, pass out the results from the customer interviews. Discuss how thinking "should" and "could" might be hindering service to the customers and restricting sales. Follow this with the sales managers' reports on their session. Lead a discussion on why people are acting the way they are using the four-quadrant activity as an illustration.

Managing Transitions. Pass out the worksheet on managing transitions (activity 6-5). Go over the model with the group and share examples of endings, the neutral zone, and new beginnings. For more information, read the book *Managing Transitions* by William Bridges. Give the participants time to quietly fill out the worksheet.

Share answers in the small teams of three to five participants. Ask each team to pick a person to share a summary of the rest of the group's responses.

Managing Stress. Through a series of worksheets, this part of the session will help each person measure his or her own stress as well as reveal what is important to him or her (as reflected in his or her lifestyle and time management). Activities 6-6, 6-7, and 6-8 contain all the worksheets you need to get through the stress management portion of the 1-day session. Pass out the worksheets and give the participants permission to go work on this activity somewhere else if being alone would help them think. Give them at least 30 minutes to compose their answers.

When people return, debrief around what they have learned by asking people to pair up and share their responses. This will take another 30 minutes. When this is complete, talk about the experience as a group:

- What surprised you about your answers?
- What did not surprise you about your answers?
- On a scale of 1 to 10 (high), what is your current stress level?

- What are some ways of reducing your stress that *are not* under your control?

- What are some ways of reducing your stress that *are* under your control?

Dealing With Burnout: Intentions Worksheet. Using the intentions worksheet (activity 6-9), ask participants again to go off by themselves and consider their goals based on their stress and time assessments. Encourage them to think through the entire worksheet to keep their lives in balance.

Tips. Try these ideas to make the workshop run smoothly:

- Remember that this is a highly individual, reflective day. This is not the strength of most salespeople. Give them plenty of time to share their results but in a way that keeps them safe (small groups or one-on-one). To process effectively, they will have to process socially.

- Devoting too much time to these activities is better than not enough. Do not rush these reflections.

- Be sure that the instructions are clear when you send people out to reflect, especially about what time you want them to return.

Results. If at first people are reluctant to share their responses with the group (as this information is very personal in many cases), you must be persistent. Eventually a few people will share their observations, and then everyone becomes engaged. People are scared—scared of being fired, scared that the company is going under, and scared that they will not be able to get another job.

By moving to the intentions stage, people are given the power to control a little bit of their destiny. You have emphasized that no one can control change, but everyone can control how he or she reacts to it.

Customizing Tips. If you don't have as much time, consider assigning the worksheets as a prerequisite. Be prepared for what you will do when people show up without the worksheets filled out.

If you do not have access to the customer, consider using people who work directly with the customer like implementation teams or call center personnel.

Measuring Your Success

To measure ongoing improvement, consider the following:

- Encourage the sales managers to review their staff members' intentions, and revisit their progress at least every 30 days. To build even more trust, have the sales managers share their own intentions with their team.

- Consider continuing customer interviews yearly to check on overall service perception. Another alternative to ensure buy-in is to have the sales managers do the customer calls periodically and share the results with not only the other sales managers, but also their teams.

Debrief

Change is not only a constant today, it is an accelerating constant. Many teams benefit from having better models to understand their own and others' abilities to thrive during change. This sales organization has never had the opportunity to grieve for the old ways or see the possibilities in the new ways. The staff have been thrown into a place that is uncomfortable, and each person is struggling.

Notice in this story, that if you didn't listen well to the situation, you might have assumed that these folks need sales training. Turns out, it isn't the sales technique that is the biggest problem, it is the salespeople's lack of discipline in applying what they already know works well. They aren't able to modify their own strengths because they are very busy fighting change on a psychological level.

Also, notice that when an organization places increased pressure on salespeople, raising the bar each pay cycle with no new customers or product, the team will eventually give up. It is not uncommon for sales organizations to go through ups and downs due to this common corporate mistake. Help salespeople by giving them new things to challenge them instead of penalizing them for doing well by asking for more.

In the next chapter, the organization is struggling with a national change—the need to audit and prove compliance to corporate and federal policies. In days past, it has been enough to show that someone attended a class on a new regulation or rule. Now, under the present regulatory milieu, organizations must also prove that learning occurred and behaviors are being monitored. This is great for the Training Triage Master!

Activity 6-1. Customer interview questions.

When you meet with the customers, begin a discussion around these questions:

- As a valued customer, we'd like your feedback on how our service to you can be improved. How would you describe your business with your salesperson?
- How would you describe your business with the implementation team?
- How would you describe your business when you call our staff with questions or concerns?
- Do you feel our service to you is improving? Why or why not?

Activity 6-1

Activity 6-2. Sales management interview questions.

When you meet with the sales managers, begin a discussion around these questions:

- What have you seen that indicates that the sales staff is struggling?
- How does your sales staff describe the firings that just occurred?
- How have you explained these firings to the sales staff?
- What is the effect of the current hiring freeze?
- What are the behaviors and symptoms that point to sales staff burnout?
- What is creating the situation that the sales staff cannot be replaced for 6 months?
- How many customers have stopped doing business with the company?
- What is the seniority of the sales staff?
- What was the retention rate before the firings began?

Activity 6-2

Activity 6-3. Mini assessment.

1. How good do you think our service is for our customers? (1 low to 10 high)

   1 2 3 4 5 6 7 8 9 10

2. How satisfied are you with your job? (1 low to 10 high)

   1 2 3 4 5 6 7 8 9 10

Activity 6-3

Activity 6-4. The four-quadrant exercise.

Activity 6-4

Activity 6-5. Managing transitions worksheet.

Describe the change that has occurred.

Rate the following emotions you are feeling due to this change. A rating of 1 means "not experiencing" and 4 means "experiencing."

Part 1

Denial	1 2 3 4
Anger	1 2 3 4
Fear	1 2 3 4
Shock	1 2 3 4
Frustration	1 2 3 4
PART 1 TOTAL:	_____

Part 2

Confusion	1 2 3 4
Stress	1 2 3 4
Creativity	1 2 3 4
Skepticism	1 2 3 4
PART 2 TOTAL:	_____

Part 3

Acceptance	1 2 3 4
Impatience	1 2 3 4
Hope	1 2 3 4
Energy	1 2 3 4
Excitement	1 2 3 4
PART 3 TOTAL:	_____

What is the most significant emotion you are experiencing at this time? What is your thought process that is generating this emotion?

Activity 6-5, page 1

What are some things that you will lose because of this change? What are you beginning to grieve for that you will not have any more?

Write a brief obituary for the things you will lose.

What are some things that you will gain because of this change? What do you hope you will get that you don't have now? What emotion does that thought trigger?

Write a brief birth announcement for the things you will gain.

Activity 6-5, page 2

Activity 6-6. Managing stress.

Complete the following table:

Category	Ideal	Reality	Gap
Work			
Family			
Health			
Possessions			
Finance			
Spiritual			
Friends			

Complete the following matrix:

What do you have that you want?	What do you have that you don't want?
What do you not have that you want?	What do you not have that you don't want?

Action Plan:

1. What will you do to help yourself manage the symptoms of stress?

2. What will you do to help yourself manage the gap between "real" and "ideal"—the cause of your stress?

Activity 6-6

Activity 6-7. Life priorities.

Complete the following table, filling in the two most important examples of each of the categories (for example, the two people most important to you):

A person	A person
A possession	A possession
What you are good at	What you are good at
A hobby you enjoy	A hobby you enjoy

Round 1
Pretend your job suddenly requires a great deal of overtime. Which two do you choose to give up?

Round 2
Pretend that you have a close relative who has health issues that require your immediate attention. Which two (in addition to those eliminated in round 1) do you give up now?

Round 3
Pretend that you have health issues that require your immediate attention. Which two (in addition to those eliminated in rounds 1 and 2) do you give up now?

Round 4
Pretend that your health issues have become so difficult that you must give up one of the remaining two things. What would it be?

Activity 6-7, page 1

Rank (prioritize) the following things from most important (#1) to least (#10)

_____ Children
_____ Extended family
_____ Faith/prayer
_____ Friends
_____ Health
_____ Money/possessions
_____ Philanthropy
_____ Power/status
_____ Spouse
_____ Work

Reflection: What surprised you about these exercises?

Activity 6-7, page 2

Activity 6-8. Life priorities pie chart.

Using the pie chart below, reflect on how you spend your time over a full week (100 percent). Fill in the percentage of time spent on each of the following:

_____ Children
_____ Extended family
_____ Faith/prayer
_____ Friends
_____ Health
_____ Money/possessions
_____ Philanthropy
_____ Power/status
_____ Spouse
_____ Work
100% TOTAL

Reflection: What surprised you about this exercise?

Redraw the pie chart after comparing your time spent to your ideal priorities from activity 6-7. In an ideal world, how would you like to spend your time?

Activity 6-8

Activity 6-9. Intentions.

Based on your life priorities and goals for spending time in alignment with these priorities, write down some intentions (at least one per category) for the following categories using these guidelines:

- Use the present tense for your statements.
- Make sure your intentions are measurable.
- Identify the emotions associated with the intention.

Note: The first row is completed for you as an example.

Category	Behavior	Measure	Emotions	Intention Statement
Children	I read bedtime stories to my children...	...at least three times a week	Joy Belonging Love	I experience joy and love when I read bedtime stories to my children at least three times a week.
Children				
Extended family				
Faith/Prayer				
Friends				
Health				
Money/Possessions				
Philanthropy				
Power/Status				
Spouse				
Work				

Activity 6-9

chapter 7

Compliance Training

What's Sarbanes-Oxley Anyway?

An executive from a large manufacturing company has called you. The company has invested heavily in shoring up its financial and accounting procedures to comply with the requirements of the Sarbanes-Oxley Act. However, the company must be able to prove in court, if need be, that the entire company was trained, knowledgeable, and held accountable for these new processes.

What They Say—The Situation

You: What has happened that triggered this call?

Executive: As you know, with Enron and WorldCom and other companies that have cooked their books, the government passed a law called Sarbanes-Oxley that requires companies to adhere to certain accounting and reporting standards. We have spent the last 2 years bringing our software and processes in line with these standards. The next step is to train all our employees on how these new systems and processes will affect them.

You: So, it sounds like you need training on the systems and process changes.

Executive: Yes, but that's not enough. It's not like training we've done in the past. We need to measure that not only did they attend the training, but also we need to be able to prove that they learned the material. We also need to prove that their behaviors are being monitored through their performance reviews. In other words, we have to be able to show that our employees have learned and are using the new processes. Not only that, but we have to have the systems in place to show that when employees failed to learn and apply their learning, we took action.

You: It sounds like the managers are going to be a critical component of this. How will the performance review change?

Executive: The actual process of the performance review will not change. There will be additional competencies relating to the new processes and systems that individuals have not been assessed against before. These will be on all job descriptions—top to bottom—and will vary depending on the responsibilities of each job. Managers will have to improve their coaching and observation to surpass former standards. Goals must be set and monitored and documented. Improvement, or lack thereof, must be carefully documented as well. These processes are not optional, and staff that do not adhere to them put the company at risk. If employees do not adopt the processes, we will have to let them go.

What You Hear

Your conversation with the client and your research has brought you to the conclusions outlined on table 7-1.

You build agreement with the executive that the goals of the compliance program are the following:

1. Train the entire company on the new Sarbanes-Oxley processes and system changes.

2. Train managers on coaching and performance review expectations, including documentation.

3. Set up a process for measuring and reporting training results.

Table 7-1. Logical conclusions.

What the Client Says	What You Hear
Compliance is mission critical.	Training is less of an issue than proving that learning has occurred and, if it has not, that the company did something about it.
Performance review and development opportunities will be critical.	Managers have not followed consistent processes for performance review, especially on the development opportunity end. All development activities for a staff member toward compliance must be carefully documented, a process that is new to most managers.
Everyone needs to be trained.	It is very unlikely that a company will fund face-to-face training for every employee. In addition, ongoing refresher training will be important in this situation. A blended approach makes the most sense.

Training will be rolled out from the top down; the managers will attend coaching and process training first. The staff will attend process training after their managers have completed the training.

What You Do

Begin where all good performance solutions begin—with asking the right questions. Your training and performance instincts have already given you some good guidance, but as is true for all successful interventions, you first have to figure out what's really behind what is said. Here are some questions that you should ask before the solution can be proposed:

- What are the processes the employees and managers need to be trained on? How are they documented? How is this documentation kept up to date? How are changes communicated to the staff?

- How aware are most managers of the changes coming down the road? How much do they see their jobs changing?

- How aware are most nonmanagers of the changes coming down the road? How much do they see their jobs changing?

- What do the current job descriptions look like? What will be added specifically to each job description around these compliance issues?

- Are there any training modules for coaching and performance review that can be reused?

- What are the time constraints? How long does the company have to prove compliance?

Results of Questions

In this example, you have learned several important things by asking these questions:

1. The processes are well documented, and the compliance organization owns the updating and communication of changes. The compliance staff will act as your SMEs.

2. The system changes are minor but confusing to the staff.

3. Most of the staff are aware of all the changes but only from a project standpoint. They know there have been many system and procedural changes because many of them have been involved in the implementation of these, but most do not understand the big picture—why and what it means to them.

4. There is currently no standard training on coaching and performance review that can be reused.

5. The compliance area is working on which competencies to add to the job descriptions and the performance review process; the competencies will be completed within the month.

6. There is a need for ongoing refresher training, especially as part of a developmental opportunity triggered by a poor performance review. This training will be taken one person at a time; therefore, it will need to be self-paced instead of face to face.

Your Triage Intervention

Through detailed consultations with the executive, you have identified all of the constraints of this project. These include the following:

1. The company has 600 employees at three locations. A total of $250,000 has been budgeted for this project, not including travel expenses. The company would like you to train the 150 managers face to face (all at once, if possible), and then provide the managers with training materials to teach their teams.

2. The refresher training will be conducted via e-learning. Pre- and posttesting for the live and e-learning will need to be Web-based and the results uploaded to the company's learning management system.

3. The manager's training sessions will occur in 2 months. The managers will train their teams in the next month. Refresher training will begin in 6 months.

Having thought deeply about each constraint and developing a proposal that keeps each in mind, you have developed the initiative plan shown in figure 7-1. The executive has accepted your proposal.

Figure 7-1. Your compliance training intervention.

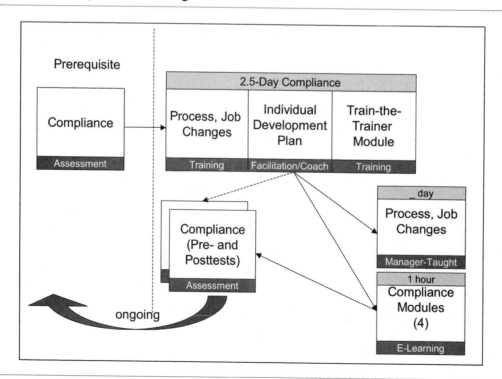

1. Off-Site Managers' Workshop

This will be a customized workshop lasting 2-1/2 days to cover all identified compliance procedures. It will cover not only the behavioral expectations and the processes, but also the systems the managers use. The new performance review and job description will be clearly explained.

In addition, managers will attend the half-day train-the-trainer session to help them deliver the compliance topics to their own teams.

2. Managers Are New Trainers

This part of the initiative is a half-day module for each manager's team to be taught by the managers. This module will be completely self-contained and will provide the manager with materials to go over the compliance issues with their team and the effects on their job descriptions and performance reviews. This module will include Web-based pre- and posttests.

3. Four 1-Hour e-Learning Modules

Each of the e-learning modules will cover the basic requirements of compliance. The PowerPoint slides from the workshop and the train-the-trainer module will be used to build e-learning modules.

What You Build

The plan is approved, and now it is time for you to design the measurable learning objectives for each part of the proposed solution, determine facilitation requirements, and create course materials. The components of your intervention are

- prerequisite compliance pretest and posttest (for all modules)
- an off-site workshop lasting 2-1/2 days for all 150 managers
- A half-day module for each manager's team to be taught by the managers
- four 1-hour e-learning modules.

4. Prerequisite Compliance Pretest and Posttest

Learning Objectives. After completing the pretest, attendees of each of the sessions will be able to identify gaps in their knowledge about compliance. Upon completing the posttest, attendees of each of the sessions will be knowledgeable about compliance. In turn, the company will have an audit trail that they have taught and tested the knowledge of all employees.

Required Equipment and Supplies. For administering the pre- and posttests, you will need the following items:

- paper forms or a Web-based assessment
- email notification (for the pretest)
- tracked email reports to make sure assessments are done on time
- printed and electronic results reports.

You can plug these competencies into a purchased application or use a Web application such as www.surveymonkey.com.

Step-by-Step Design. To design and administer the pre- and posttests, follow these steps:

1. The pre- and posttests will be multiple choice.

2. The content of these tests must map the learning objectives and course content for the modules exactly. This audit trail is critical to compliance.

3. To ensure fairness and consistency, make the posttest the same as the pretest. Simply reorder the questions.

4. Due to the serious ramifications of this testing, it is critical that the compliance staff at the company have the final sign-off on these questions.

Tips. When building multiple choice tests, ensure that the right answer varies. For example, half of the answers should not be "A" because the spread will be far too uneven. Avoid patterns if possible. Good multiple choice tests include a right answer, an almost right answer, a totally wrong answer, and a wrong answer that is a common misconception.

Top Priority

In this case, you are going to distribute the pretest results at the beginning of both the workshop and the half-day train-the-trainer module following these steps:

- Reduce anxiety by explaining to participants that the pretest is used to set learning objectives: the lower the score, the more potential learning!

- Go over the answers to each question so that the participants learn from their mistakes.

- Briefly discuss the answers when there is controversy, but push back the extended discussion until the material is taught in class.

- Explain to them that there will be a posttest using similar questions, so it is important for them to keep the pretests from which they may study.

- Build some functionality into the e-learning modules so that they can print off the pretest with the right answers.

- Track scores to show improvement between the pre- and posttests.

Results. The results of the pretests identify the areas of compliance that are least understood. The classroom time will be adjusted to fit the needs dictated by the pretest results.

Off-Site 2-1/2-Day Workshop for All Managers
The 2-1/2-day workshop will be completely customized to the needs of the client. A sample agenda is presented in activity 7-1.

When considering how long the development will take, use the following equation for instructor-led material:

Number of Hours of Instruction Time × Development Time Ratio = Total Time to Build

The development time ratio is assigned a value from 10 to 20. If it is assigned 10, the developer knows all the requirements already and there are plenty of SMEs to help. A value of 20 means the developer knows nothing about the requirements and SMEs are not easily accessible. For this example,

20 Hours of Instruction × 15 = 300 Hours of Development Time

This means the workshop will not be ready for 3 months. If you do not have that much time, consider shortcuts for development such as:

- updating existing materials that have been used in meetings or in other classes
- employing guest speakers to develop parts of the presentation with your guidance
- developing exercises for the learners to self-discover (using documentation) the compliance requirements.

Learning Objectives. After attending this session, all of the managers (to whom this workshop is targeted) will apply good compliant behaviors at all times in everything they do.

Required Equipment and Supplies. Before the workshop, assemble the following items:

- flipcharts and markers
- student guide (and supporting PowerPoint slides)
- PowerPoint projection equipment (LCD projector and screen).

Step-by-Step. Following are the steps to successfully deliver the workshop program:

1. Activity 7-1 shows a sample agenda for the workshop. Here are some ideas for teaching the materials:

    - Use the Sequence game (explained further in chapter 9 and activity 9-3) when students must learn a new process or series of steps.
    - Use coaching games (see activities 3-4 and 3-8) when students need to learn new processes for performance review and development of staff.

2. Whenever possible, use interaction to teach and rehearse new materials. Use lecture delivery as a last resort.

Tips. Check out Learningware's games for teaching compliance. The company's displayable and Web-based games (similar to "Jeopardy," "Wheel of Fortune," and "Who Wants to Be a Millionaire?") are wonderful ways to teach new information without making it boring.

Manager-Taught Half-Day Workshop

The half-day workshop will be a streamlined version of the 2-1/2-day version, completely customized to the needs of the client (activity 7-2). It will give the managers an opportunity to use the skills they learned during their private session by teaching the company staff the new compliance measures. When considering how long the development will take, use the same equation:

4 Hours of Instruction × 10 = 40 Hours of Development Time

This means the workshop will be ready in a week or two by reusing materials from the 2-1/2-day version. The hard part of this development will be pulling only a half day's worth of materials from the 2 days' worth of material. (Remember, a half day was utilized as a train-the-trainer session.)

Consider the following:

1. Resist the temptation to lecture only. It is much better if people learn less information really well, than more information really poorly, especially in compliance training.

2. Try using games or game software to reinforce the learning, keep the session lively, and maintain high retention.

3. The pre- and posttests are still required. This means you really have only 3 hours of learning time.

Learning Objectives. After attending this session, each of the employees will apply good compliant behaviors at all times in everything they do.

Required Equipment and Supplies. For this part of the intervention, you need

- flipcharts
- markers
- student guide.

Step-by-Step. Following these steps can help ensure that your workshop helps the participants meet the learning objective:

1. Activity 7-2 shows a sample agenda for the workshop. Here are some ideas for teaching the materials:

    - Use the Sequence game (discussed in chapter 9) when students must learn a new process or series of steps.

    - Use the coaching games when students need to learn new processes for performance review and development of staff.

    - Have different team members teach different parts of the workshop. Give them the materials ahead of time to learn and then have them present or lead an interaction.

2. Whenever possible, use interactive methods to teach and rehearse new materials. Lecture as a last resort.

Four 1-Hour E-Learning Modules

The four 1-hour e-learning modules will be completely customized to the needs of the client. (See the sample agenda in activity 7-3). E-learning takes much more time to develop. The development time ratio is now given a value between 20 and 30, but new resources allow you to convert existing PowerPoint tools into modules much faster. Using this type of tool, the estimate to create these four modules is

4 Hours of Instruction × 25 = 100 Hours of Development Time

This means the e-learning modules will take another 3 weeks or so to develop. Consider some shortcuts for development such as these:

- Start with the PowerPoint slides that you have. Carefully minimize the materials to just "need to know" rather than "nice to know."

- Buy animated clipart to drop into the training. The color and interaction will keep the learners' attention.

- Ensure that you have aligned the learning objectives and content to the testing standards.

Learning Objectives. After attending this session, the staff will apply good compliant behaviors at all times in everything they do.

Required Equipment and Supplies. You will need the following:

- Pre- and posttest
- Access to the software
- Student guide.

Step-by-Step.

1. Activity 7-3 shows a sample agenda for the four modules. Here are some ideas for teaching the materials:

   - Allow participants to print out their pretest and results.
   - Break the posttest into sections and do part of the test after each module.

2. Figure out how to report the results of the e-learning modules. Will the company want these results delivered as an email, a spreadsheet, an ASCII file to link into the learning management system (LMS)? Each of these formats entails different amounts of development time.

3. Think about adding stories or scenarios to the modules so people can relate to the compliance issues.

Customizing Tips. This is an example of an intervention that is completely customized. Although it is possible to use many of the facilitation techniques shared in the other chapters in this book, the compliance material will be different for each company.

Measuring Your Success

Due to federal regulation, it is critical that the documentation of the completion of training be kept including

- pre- and posttest results per person per class
- class completion and rosters
- e-learning completion by module.

Debrief

I've never known any student that was looking forward to going to compliance training. It's like hearing that the Internal Revenue Service is coming to have lunch with you! However, in these days, it is critical that a company be able to show not only that they had policies and procedures, not only that they trained people on these policies and procedures, but also that the people actually learned. This means that you will have to build an audit trail that shows that people attended and they learned the rules well before they left.

In a sense, this need for compliance is helping training mature into the corporate asset it could have been all along. As trainers, we should be the champions of measurement, the champions of following procedures, and the champions of learning that affects behaviors.

It's hard to always agree with the corporate rules, but often the needs of the many are more important than the creativity of the individual. In the next chapter, you will read about salespeople and developers who don't see eye to eye. Both believe their work is incredibly important, and both think the other group wakes up in the morning looking for ways to mess them up. How can we get people with such different perspectives to work together without losing their passion?

Activity 7-1. The 2-Day Compliance Workshop: Sample Agenda.

Pretest

Unit 1: Introduction
Introduction by Executive Sponsor
Why Now? Overview of the Strategy Behind Compliance Changes
The Sarbanes-Oxley Act and Personal Responsibility/Liability

Unit 2: Financial Compliance
Effects on Accounts Receivable, Accounts Payable, and Payroll Systems
Reporting Expenses and Assets
Accruing Dollars
Systems Impact

Unit 3: Supervision Compliance
Hiring Procedure
Coaching Performance
Documenting Performance Improvement
Promotions, Bonuses, and Raises
Dismissal Procedure
Systems Impact

Unit 4: External Vendors
Contacting Vendors
Negotiating With Vendors
Requests for Proposals, Proposals, Work Orders, and Contracts
Working With Contractors
Systems Impact

Unit 5: The Public Face
Public Relations Compliance
Media Compliance
Working With the Public Relations and Legal Departments

Unit 6: Personal Confidentiality
Non-Compete and Nondisclosure Contract Clauses
Ownership of Proprietary Materials

Unit 7: Train-the-Trainer
How People Learn
How People Remember
Using Lecture as a Last Resort

Posttest

Activity 7-1

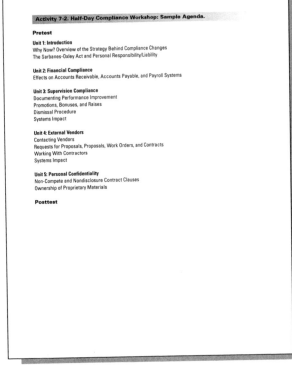

Activity 7-2. Half-Day Compliance Workshop: Sample Agenda.

Pretest

Unit 1: Introduction
Why Now? Overview of the Strategy Behind Compliance Changes
The Sarbanes-Oxley Act and Personal Responsibility/Liability

Unit 2: Financial Compliance
Effects on Accounts Receivable, Accounts Payable, and Payroll Systems

Unit 3: Supervision Compliance
Documenting Performance Improvement
Promotions, Bonuses, and Raises
Dismissal Procedure
Systems Impact

Unit 4: External Vendors
Contacting Vendors
Requests for Proposals, Proposals, Work Orders, and Contracts
Working With Contractors
Systems Impact

Unit 5: Personal Confidentiality
Non-Compete and Nondisclosure Contract Clauses
Ownership of Proprietary Materials

Posttest

Activity 7-2

Activity 7-3. E-Learning Modules: Sample Agenda.

Pretest

MODULE 1
Introduction
Why Now? Overview of the Strategy Behind Compliance Changes
The Sarbanes-Oxley Act and Personal Responsibility/Liability
Financial Compliance
Effects on Accounts Receivable, Accounts Payable, and Payroll Systems

MODULE 2
Documenting Performance Improvement
Promotions, Bonuses, and Raises
Dismissal Procedure
Systems Impact

MODULE 3
Contacting Vendors
Requests for Proposals, Proposals, Work Orders, and Contracts
Working With Contractors
Systems Impact

MODULE 4
Personal Confidentiality
Non-Compete and Nondisclosure Contract Clauses
Ownership of Proprietary Materials

Posttest

Activity 7-3

► **chapter 8**

Collaboration

You Can't Promise That?

The manager of a project office at a large software company called you. She would like to talk to you about a problem involving a lack of trust between the developers of the software and the salespeople who are selling it.

What They Say—The Situation

You: What has happened that triggered this call?

Executive: We sell a Web application to doctors' offices. It is a pretty expensive application and requires our sales staff to build strong, trusting relationships first to make the sale and later to keep the business. We also have a highly skilled group of developers who are writing the software. For each implementation, there is a great deal of customization done so that it fits easily into the doctor's current office setting, which is why the system is so expensive.

There's always been a tension between the salespeople and the developers. Lately, our business is growing, which is a good thing, but the tension has grown to a point where it is causing project delays, which, in at least one case, lost us a customer.

You: So, it sounds like the salespeople and the developers are having trouble getting along. What are some of the gripes they have about each other?

Executive: Standard stuff, really. The developers believe that the salespeople never say no. They blame the developers for promising more than the developers could ever get done on time. The salespeople think the developers are barriers to meeting the customers' needs. I think the salespeople don't really understand what the developers do and the developers don't really understand what the salespeople do. It's natural to think that your job is more complicated than anyone else's.

You: So, they may not be getting along, at least in part, because one group doesn't understand what the other group needs. What other things might be discouraging them from collaborating?

Executive: Well, they are rewarded for different things. The developers are rewarded for getting the systems in on time, and the salespeople are rewarded for making the sale. Maybe this is part of the problem.

What You Hear

Your conversation with the client and your research has brought you to the conclusions identified in table 8-1.

Table 8-1. Logical conclusions.

What the Client Says	What You Hear
The developers and the sales staff are not getting along.	I don't know how to help them to get along. They pretend to get along in my presence, but it is obvious with the project troubles we are experiencing that they are not communicating at all.
Sales are growing, and projects are failing.	This problem has existed since the beginning. I could ignore this before we got this busy, but the heat is on since we've started to miss deadlines.

You build agreement with the executive that the goals of the collaboration program are the following:

- Encourage collaboration between sales and development by helping them learn more about what the other group needs and by encouraging trust.

- Define joint incentives to encourage the developers and salespeople to work together.

What You Do

Begin where all good performance solutions begin—with asking the right questions. Your training and performance instincts have already given you some good guidance, but as is true for all successful interventions, it is necessary that you first figure out what's really behind what is said. Here are some questions that need to be asked before the solution can be proposed:

- What types of behavioral changes would you like to see after the program is completed? What behaviors by the salespeople and developers would indicate improvement?

- What kind of metrics can be included to encourage sales and development to work together? How can the company help the salespeople to set better boundaries with the customer? How can the developers react to change more quickly and accurately?

- What is in the job descriptions for sales and development? Are they appraised for their ability to collaborate with each other?

Results of Questions

In this example, you have learned the following by asking these questions:

- There is no incentive for collaboration between sales and development. The executive is interested in adding competencies to each department's job descriptions to practice collaboration.

- Part of the session will be dedicated to getting the sales and development staff to work together to build new ways to work together. By generating some of these ideas themselves, there will be more ownership.

- This behavior has been accepted by the company for many years. There are established patterns of "us versus them" in these organizations.

Your Triage Intervention

The executive has outlined a list of constraints around which your project must be facilitated:

- Because of project load, there will need to be two sessions with 10 people in each one. (There are 10 salespeople and 10 developers in all.) The executive will kick off each session but will not stay.

- The job description changes will be made before class. These will take 1 month to implement.

- The sessions will be conducted back to back to ensure that everyone hears the same message at about the same time.

- The managers will facilitate a 1-hour summary meeting for their teams so that information can be shared from both sessions. The executive will attend each of these as well.

What You Build

You have proposed to the executive the plan laid out in figure 8-1 and she has accepted.

- Prerequisite assessment for the sales and development staff to evaluate each other's collaboration (activity 8-1). **Purpose:** Establish language for open discussion.

- A 1-day face-to-face workshop. **Purpose:** Review survey results and establish the problem.
  — Opposites brainstorming (activity 8-2)

Figure 8-1. Your collaboration intervention.

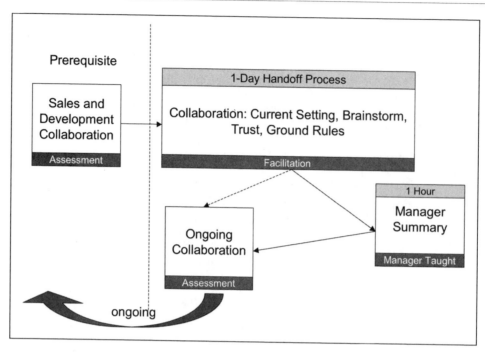

— Saboteur simulation exercise (activity 8-3)

— Ground rules for success (activity 8-4). **Purpose:** Establish buy-in, set roles, and develop a process for ongoing collaboration.

■ Script for the 1-hour manager meeting to combine workshop participants and debrief (activity 8-5). **Purpose:** Ensure consistent discussion and ongoing adoption of new collaborative process.

You will deliver the sessions in 2 months. More details on your intervention appear in the following sections.

1. Prerequisite Assessment

In this situation, the assessment (activity 8-1) will be used to compare the results of the sales staff's perception of development collaboration to the development's perception of the sales staff's collaboration. The survey is for the sales and development staff to assess the collaboration between the two. This data will be used to start the workshop.

2. The 1-Day Face-to-Face Workshop

The workshop will get salespeople to learn about each other, helping to reduce preconceived notions and the prevailing us-against-them mentality. Initially, the results of the prerequisite survey will be presented and discussed. Then mixed teams will brainstorm using the Opposites technique (activity 8-2). After brainstorming about how to make collaboration worse, the teams will flip the results to actions to improve collaboration. Then the teams will play the Saboteur card game (activity 8-3), examining how lack of trust affects team behavior. Finally, the developers and sales staff will work together to establish ground rules for success (activity 8-4).

3. A 1-Hour Manager Meeting

Because the teams will attend in two different sessions, the managers will bring their entire teams together to share results from both sessions to ensure that the teams have a shared experience (activity 8-5). These meetings will be scripted to help the managers keep them consistent across all groups. The main purpose is to combine all the workshop participants and then debrief after the day's activities.

The Prerequisite Survey

Learning Objectives. After completing this assessment and sharing the results in class, the sales and development staff will clearly identify the extent of their collaboration problem.

Required Equipment and Supplies. For the survey, you will need the following:

- paper forms or a Web-based assessment
- email notification of the prerequisite assessment
- printed and electronic versions of the results reports.

You can plug these competencies into a purchased application, use a Web application such as www.surveymonkey.com, or do the surveys using email or paper. The choice depends on your budget and the number of survey participants. It is critical to ensure that the results will remain completely anonymous and that they are presented only in summary form for the two groups (sales and development). The language asking the participant for their department must be *very* clear. If participants choose the wrong department, it can be difficult to draw any meaningful conclusions from the results.

Step-by-Step Design. You follow these steps to guide the development of this part of your intervention:

1. Write the assessment questions and ask the executive sponsor for approval.

2. Send the assessment to each participant.

3. Be specific about the date the assessment will close. Track the number of assessments done a week before the assessment is closed, and email reminders to the people who have yet to complete it.

4. Make both electronic and hard copy versions of the results report to give to management and to the participants at their workshop.

One-Day Workshop

Learning Objectives. After completing this 1-one day workshop, the participants will be able to:

- implement actions to increase their personal collaboration with the other department

■ assess their own barriers to collaboration and correct them

■ appreciate the challenges of the other department so that partnering can occur.

Required Equipment and Supplies. For this workshop, you will need the following items available:

■ blank paper

■ flipchart paper

■ colored markers

■ two decks of cards for every five participants

■ the results reports from the prerequisite assessment.

Step-by-Step Design. You then follow these steps to guide the development of this part of your intervention:

1. Welcome everyone to the session. Allow people to sit where they want, but build teams of three to five participants. It is very likely that the teams will be drawn across departmental lines. Begin by passing out the results of the surveys.

2. Ask each person to read through the reports silently.

3. Ask each participant to pick one strength and one weakness that are shown by the results, and have participants share these thoughts in their small groups. They should share a story of a specific time when collaboration succeeded because of a strength. Ask the team to help brainstorm why the situation went well.

4. Ask each person to share an example of a time when collaboration struggled because of the weakness chosen. Ask the team to help brainstorm other ways the situation could have been handled.

5. Be prepared to share one strength and one weakness story with the entire group.

Brainstorming Opposites. You will now break people into new teams for the Opposites brainstorming (activity 8-2). At this point, ask people to get in teams that are mixed—half sales and half development. If this is hard to do, consider dividing them up yourself.

1. Give each team a large piece of flipchart paper to lay on the table and a handful of colored markers (enough so that each person has one). Ask them to brainstorm ways to make the collaboration problem worse. They can use the markers to write words or draw to express their ideas. They can add to other people's words if they want. Let them brainstorm for 10 minutes.

2. Have each team send half of the participants (which should be half development and half sales) to another table. Continue brainstorming by writing on the pieces of paper. Let this brainstorming go on for 10 minutes.

3. Have each team send the group that hasn't moved yet to a different table (and not the table to which their ex-teammates have moved). At this point, ask the teams to brainstorm on a new piece of flipchart paper ways to turn the opposite ideas into positives. For example, "stop talking to each other" becomes "communicate constantly." Let this brainstorming continue for 15 minutes.

4. Ask the teams to post this positive flipchart on the wall.

5. Each individual will now go around the room and add to any flipchart he or she cares to add to. Make sure every flipchart is visited.

6. Ask the original creators to move back to their flipchart. Ask them to share one favorite yet unique (not shared yet) idea from their flipchart, either one they came up with or one someone added to their chart. As the teams share this idea, gather them on a central flipchart at the front of the room.

Saboteur Simulation. The previous exercises have been strongly social and probably seem to be successful, but it takes an exercise with competition to provoke people to display some of the behaviors that are really breaking down communication. In this game (activity 8-3), teams will compete to sort decks of cards as quickly as possible. To do this, teams must create a shared view of the process, and participate collaboratively. You will throw a wrench into the activity by placing saboteurs on some of the teams. Ideally, you want the teams to be organized in the following ways:

- one team thinks it has a saboteur but does not
- one team thinks it has a saboteur and does
- one team has a saboteur but thinks it does not
- one team doesn't have a saboteur and doesn't think it does.

Pass out the cards from activity 8-3 to organize participants this way. Explain they cannot share these cards.

1. Clearly explain that the race will be to sort shuffled decks of cards into sequenced decks of cards. The team that can correctly sort the most decks in 2 minutes wins. Write this definition of sorting on the board: "Sorting means ace (low) to king (high), hearts, diamonds, clubs, spades."

2. Explain that any saboteur who is not discovered will win a prize and any person accused of being a saboteur but who is not will win a prize. This will amplify the lack of trust.

3. Begin the race. Try to watch the saboteurs so it is easier for you to catch the mess they make of the deck.

4. After 2 minutes, announce the winner and hand out the prizes. Ask each team to decide if they had a saboteur and to identify who it is. Give prizes if they are right or wrong. Give the saboteur the opportunity to tell what he or she was doing to befuddle the team. Give the team members the opportunity to tell why they thought someone was a saboteur if the person wasn't.

Tips. To debrief this exercise, ask the following:

- What caused you to question others' actions? What assumptions did you make about saboteurs?

- How did your productivity change when you thought you had a saboteur?

- How did your productivity change when you were sure you did not have a saboteur?

- What happens when you go into a project expecting noncollaborative behaviors?

- How is this like or unlike the relationship between sales and development staff?

Capture these thoughts on flipchart paper to be shared later as part of the ground rules exercise.

Ground Rules for Success. At this point, review all the activities and results that have presented themselves during the day. Ask people to share any additional thoughts as you add these to the flipchart.

1. Break into new teams of three or four people. Again, ask that the teams be mixed with both development and salespeople.

2. Using activity 8-4, ask the teams to create a list of 10 ground rules for success on flipchart paper. Give them at least 20 minutes to do this.

3. Ask the teams to validate their list against the lessons learned in this session on the flipchart pages. Give them another 5 minutes to adjust their answers.

4. Ask each team to post their list of 10 rules on flipchart paper on the wall.

5. Each person will individually vote on their 10 favorite rules. Using their marker, participants will have 10 check marks to vote with. They can put one check mark by 10 different rules, all 10 next to one rule, or any combination thereof. Encourage the individuals to read every flipchart before voting. This takes at least 15 minutes.

6. Create the final list of ground rules on a piece of flipchart paper at the front of the room after discussing any ties or concerns. It may be necessary to vote more than once for tie-breakers.

7. Ask everyone to sign the rules.

Scripted Manager Meeting. This activity entails only two steps:

1. Create and pass out the script for the manager's follow-up meeting (activity 8-5). Explain that you will email them the results from each phase of the workshop.

2. Ask each person to read through the follow-up meeting script and ask any questions he or she may have about it. Close by asking each participant to share one conclusion or breakthrough achieved during the workshop.

You can customize the manager's script according to other objectives that the sponsor wants to accomplish. Keep in mind that at some point, someone will have to combine the two lists of ground rules and distribute the consolidated list to all teams before the manager's meeting. There will probably be redundancy, so if possible, reduce the list to between 10 and 15 statements to keep it manageable. Finally, consider asking the client to have posters made of the ground rules and wallet cards to keep the commitment fresh.

Measuring Your Success

The best way to check how collaboration is going is to redo the survey after 6 months and then once a year. Consider reinforcing the behavior through ongoing manager meetings.

Debrief

Finding out that developers and salespeople don't get along is never a surprise. If you look at the typical behavioral profiles of these two groups, you can predict the conflict. Ironically, the strengths of one group are often the weaknesses of the other, but together, they make an effective company. They need each other to be successful.

Of course, the two groups will never admit this. The initial assessment gives them the opportunity to take their best shots. The stereotyping and assumptions will come out loud and clear. Be careful as you debrief this activity because it could easily degrade and generate more conflict and mistrust. Make sure that the supervisors are doing everything they can to break down the stereotypes, because often they are the drivers of the group competition.

To supplement this session, you might add behavioral assessment as a prerequisite. That way, the participants confirm through their own choices, the strengths and weaknesses that define their collaboration.

In the next chapter, the conflict involves everyone in a company and a small group that is trying to implement a new way of doing things. At every attempt to put a new, repeatable process into a business, roadblocks emerge from every corner. It is impossible to move intercompany groups—be they development and sales or staff and corporate headquarters—toward collaboration without dealing with the history before the future.

Activity 8-1. Salespeople's and developers' assessments of each other.

Your role:

☐ Developer   ☐ Salesperson

Rate the person being assessed in terms of each of the characteristics listed below by circling a number from 1 (indicating no skill in the characteristic) to 6 (perfect skills in the characteristic).

Developers Competency	
Persists in managing and overcoming adversity	1 2 3 4 5 6
Prioritizes tasks and manages time effectively	1 2 3 4 5 6
Participates and contributes fully as a team member	1 2 3 4 5 6
Demonstrates empathy and understanding	1 2 3 4 5 6
Builds trust and demonstrates trustworthiness	1 2 3 4 5 6
Expresses intention clearly and concisely in written communications	1 2 3 4 5 6
Builds collaboration and clearly articulates intention in verbal communications	1 2 3 4 5 6
Understands and applies customer needs and expectations	1 2 3 4 5 6
Gathers customer requirements and input	1 2 3 4 5 6
Partners with other groups in gathering requirements, maintaining communication flow, and managing work	1 2 3 4 5 6
Takes a holistic view by thinking in terms of the entire system and the effects and consequences of actions and decisions	1 2 3 4 5 6
Operates with an awareness of marketplace competition and general landscape of related business arenas	1 2 3 4 5 6
Possesses general business acumen—functions of strategic planning, finance, marketing, manufacturing, research and development, and so on	1 2 3 4 5 6
Sets, communicates, and monitors project milestones and objectives	1 2 3 4 5 6
Prioritizes and allocates resources	1 2 3 4 5 6
Manages multiple, potentially conflicting priorities across various and diverse disciplines	1 2 3 4 5 6
Gathers and analyzes appropriate data and input and manages "noise" of information overload	1 2 3 4 5 6
Manages risk versus reward and return-on-investment equations	1 2 3 4 5 6
Balances established standards with need for exceptions in decision making	1 2 3 4 5 6
Aligns decisions with needs of the business organization and team values	1 2 3 4 5 6
Makes timely decisions in alignment with customer and business pace	1 2 3 4 5 6
Facilitates win-win solutions	1 2 3 4 5 6
Demonstrates and builds resilience in the face of change	1 2 3 4 5 6

Activity 8-1

Activity 8-2. Opposites worksheet.

Step 1

In the first column of the chart below, brainstorm as many ways as you can to answer this question:

"How can this company increase the disconnect between the salespeople and the project managers?"

Note: If you are laughing, you are doing this right. The first row is completed for you as an example.

How to Increase the Disconnect	Opposite
Example: Physically locate the salespeople in a different time zone.	Build regular communication between the teams.

Step 2

Using the right-hand column of the table, think of the opposite of the idea you have laughed about in the left-hand column. In other words, how can you use the idea on the left and transform it to the opposite to *reduce* the disconnect?

Activity 8-2

Activity 8-3. Saboteur worksheet.

Instructor Notes:

Create the following cards for teams of three to five people, keeping in mind that you will need one card for each person on the team:

Team Member's Card	TEAM 1:	TEAM 2:	TEAM 3:	TEAM 4:
	• Has a saboteur • Thinks it has a saboteur	• Has a saboteur • Thinks it does not have a saboteur	• Does not have a saboteur • Thinks it has a saboteur	• Does not have a saboteur • Thinks it does not have a saboteur
Team Member 1	You are a saboteur	You are a saboteur	Your team has a saboteur	Your team does not have a saboteur
Team Member 2	Your team has a saboteur	Your team does not have a saboteur	Your team has a saboteur	Your team does not have a saboteur
Team Member 3 (and any additional team members)	Your team has a saboteur	Your team does not have a saboteur	Your team has a saboteur	Your team does not have a saboteur

Your team will compete in a race to sort decks of cards as quickly as possible. The race will go for 5 minutes. You will sort the cards so that the ace is face up on the top of the deck and the suits progress from the top down in this order:

1. Spades
2. Clubs
3. Hearts
4. Diamonds

You will receive a card that tells you whether you have a saboteur on your team.

Activity 8-3

Activity 8-4. Sample ground rules for success.

Your team will work together to create ground rules for success. Use the following categories to clearly define measurable rules:

- Meetings

- Email

- Voicemail

- Escalation Procedures

- Issue Communication

- Chain of Command

- Status Reporting

- Other:

Activity 8-4

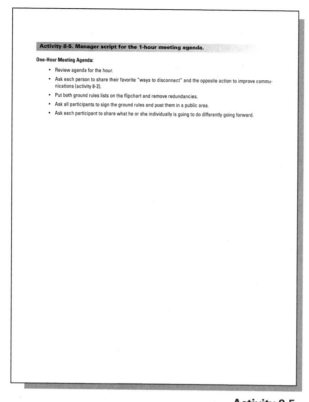

Activity 8-5. Manager script for the 1-hour meeting agenda.

One-Hour Meeting Agenda:

- Review agenda for the hour.
- Ask each person to share their favorite "ways to disconnect" and the opposite action to improve communications (activity 8-2).
- Put both ground rules lists on the flipchart and remove redundancies.
- Ask all participants to sign the ground rules and post them in a public area.
- Ask each participant to share what he or she individually is going to do differently going forward.

Activity 8-5

chapter 9

Project Management

Put First Things First

The head of a project office has contacted you. The office staff have recently purchased and modified a new methodology for project management that will be implemented across the entire company. He would like to get your help with the training on this new methodology.

What They Say—The Situation

You: What has happened that triggered this call?

Executive: I was hired by the company a year ago to standardize the project management process. Over the last year, I have opened a project office to coordinate and document project status and created an executive project dashboard of all the critical projects. Recently we have chosen a new methodology for project management. Working with a taskforce of senior project managers from our company, the vendor is putting the finishing touches on customizing the methodology for our specific needs. The vendor does have generic training available on the methodology, but I would like a 1-day workshop that all employees involved with project management will attend. The goal of the workshop would be not only to sell the standardization concept, but also to point out how the generic methods and our methods will be slightly different. Afterward, our staff can use the e-learning provided by the vendor.

You: So, the 1-day kickoff session will be an overview of the methodology including the customization done for your company, right?

Executive: Yes, but underlying it all, I need you to convince people that adhering to this new method is in their best interest. This company has had methodologies come and go in the past, and people probably will be pretty cynical about this one.

You: What are the benefits of a standard project management methodology to your people and to your company?

Executive: For the company, having a standard approach and language for projects allows us to be able to track status more accurately and move resources from project to project with less ramp-up time. For the staff, the methodology will give them a language for communicating across departments, making it easier to plan and estimate their work. It will also give people more opportunity to try new kinds of project work.

What You Hear

Your conversation with the client and your research has brought you to the conclusions listed in table 9-1.

Table 9-1. Logical conclusions.

What the Client Says	What You Hear
Request for a specific type of training.	It seems like I need customized methodology training but building a positive expectation of this methodology is really more important than learning details about what's in it.
Methodologies have come and gone.	The staff is a little jaded. They've seen methodologies come and go. The best I can hope for is that they will adopt a wait-and-see attitude, but I need more staff buy-in than that.
The vendor has generic training available.	I would like to use you for the customized kickoff, but the rest of the training will be done through the vendor's self-paced generic training materials.

You build agreement with the executive that the goals of the project management program are to sell project management staff on the new methodology and its benefits to the company and to them specifically, and to teach project management staff an overview of the new methodology (pointing them to the resources they need for more detailed learning as they need it).

What You Do

Begin where all good performance solutions begin—with asking the right questions. Your training and performance instincts have already given you some good guidance, but as is the case for all successful interventions, you first have to figure out what's really behind what is said. Here are some questions that need to be asked before the solution can be proposed:

- How can I learn the details of the generic methodology and of the vendor's customization?

- Who participated in the selection of the methodology? May I talk with them to understand more about their choice and justification?

- How many other methodologies have there been? What happened to each one?

- What role will the project office staff play in methodology rollout?

- What are other resources available to project staff when they first use the methodology other than training?

- What incentive is there for project staff to adopt this methodology?

Results of Questions

In this example, you learn from asking these questions that:

- There is currently no incentive for project staff to follow the methodology, but it will be added to their performance reviews in the next cycle.

- Two other methodologies have been rolled out in the last 15 years. The first was a homegrown methodology that was very high level and was adopted pretty well. The second was chosen to fill in the detail left out of the homegrown methodology, but it required extensive reliance on reams of documentation. Therefore, the staff resisted using it.

- The project office will serve as internal consultants on the methodology. They are available to help project teams kick off projects and troubleshoot after the projects have started.

- There is complete online documentation on the customized methodology. There are also job aids available from the vendor that can be used in class.

Your Triage Intervention

During additional in-depth discussions, the executive has outlined the constraints around which your training must function. First, a walkthrough on the 1-day workshop will be scheduled in 2 months and will be attended by the project office staff, the taskforce, and the executive. In addition, the 1-day workshop will be rolled out after modifications (if needed) within 3 months. All project staff will attend this workshop over 3 months. There will be 25 people per class, and the goal is to mix project and product teams to create a more diverse group.

Keeping the aforementioned wishes of the executive in mind, you have proposed the plan depicted in figure 9-1 and he has accepted.

- A 1-day workshop on the customized methodology. **Purpose:** Overcome the bad reputations of the old methodologies, explain the new

Figure 9-1. Your project management intervention.

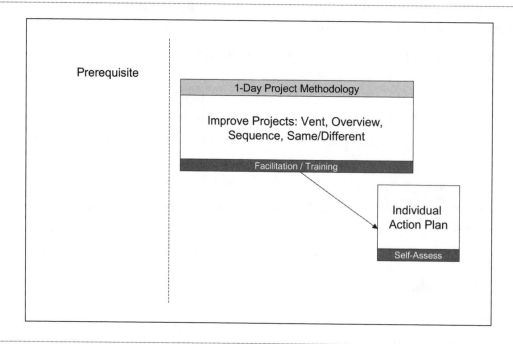

methodology, and promote adoption of the project management methodology by all staff. The intervention will involve the following activities:

- *Venting:* Recall old methodologies and their problems, then create action plans to avoid repeating mistakes (activity 9-1).

- *Overview:* Introduce the methodology phases with the job aid and a mnemonic for each of the phases (activity 9-2).

- *Sequence:* Play a card game to sequence the project phases and deliverables (activity 9-3).

- *Same/Different:* Brainstorm ideas on how to screw up the adoption of the methodology, and then brainstorm ideas on how the methodology will improve project work (activity 9-4).

- *Personal Action Plan:* Activity 9-5 presents a sample project office contract.

- *Resources:* A table of all the resources for ongoing learning is available as activity 9-6.

More details about the solution are offered in the following sections.

1. Venting

Inexperienced trainers often use brilliant delivery techniques to avoid negative emotions in a classroom. Activity 9-1 allows participants to explore and relive memories of unsuccessful methodologies and create action plans to ensure these mistakes aren't repeated. It is not unusual to be in a situation where the participants have entered the room feeling angry or at least concerned. Ignoring these emotions will doom the learning experiences. Instead, it is critical in performance consulting to acknowledge the negative emotions right off the bat. This venting exercise will give participants a safe way to express their feelings and help them take appropriate action to improve the situation.

2. Overview

The easiest way to introduce new processes and methodologies—especially project management—is to organize the phases in simple, easy-to-remember chunks and then wrap a metaphor around the whole thing.

In this case, the methodology is to be presented as four distinct phases, represented by the mnemonic "Dare to Properly Manage Resources," with the first letter of each word representing the first letter of the four phases: Define, Plan, Manage, Review (activity 9-2). A job aid can help people grasp the most important deliverables of each of the phases. Presented this way, a methodology seems so commonsensical that it is difficult for anyone to raise any arguments. In addition, this high-level view implies that there is plenty of room for individual skill and creativity, a common concern when adopting new processes.

3. Sequence

This game (activity 9-3) is based on a children's game in which participants compete to get their cards into sequence. The trick is this: On each turn, a player has to draw a card and discard a card. The only way to sequence out-of-order cards is to replace them with new cards, and the first person to complete his or her sequence wins.

All methodologies comprise a sequence of activities, deliverables, and phases. In this case, there are only four phases, so that wouldn't make much of a game. In project management, what you deliver is more critical than the activity you performed to deliver; therefore, the game focuses around the deliverables. The cards are based on the deliverables from the job aid. As they play, participants have to discuss the order in which things occur, creating multiple opportunities to learn and review without even noticing.

4. Same/Different

This is a two-part brainstorming technique (activity 9-4). In the first round, participants in teams are asked to brainstorm ways to screw up the adoption of the methodology. The team earns a point for any unique answer it comes up with. Second, participants in the same teams are asked to brainstorm ways to ensure that the methodology will improve project work quickly. Notice that this statement is basically the opposite of the first but rephrased to encourage deeper thinking and a new perspective. In round two, teams get a point for every answer that they have that another team also has, encouraging a shared vision of what is needed for future success.

5. Personal Action Plan: Contract With the Project Office

This is the part of the facilitation where you get a personal commitment from each participant that he or she will participate in the adoption of the methodology in a positive and productive way. Up to this point, you have set the stage for participants to learn the methodology at a high level. You have encouraged them to get involved in figuring out how to make the methodology successful. This contract (activity 9-5) makes the participation real and concrete.

6. Resources

Finally, the participants will be given a list of resources (activity 9-6) to learn more about the methodology when they are using it. This will include training options, the project office's services, documentation (preferably online), and sample project options. If possible, participants will have an opportunity to play with these resources before they leave.

What You Build

The plan is approved, and now it is time for you to design the measurable learning objectives for each part of the proposed solution, determine facilitation requirements, and create course materials. The details for each follow.

Venting

Learning Objectives. After completing this experience, the participant will be able to express and acknowledge negative emotions and fears from previous experiences with methodologies. Also, participants should be able to contrast past experiences with methodologies to the plans for this methodology. Lastly, they should adopt a wait-and-see attitude about the use of this methodology.

Required Equipment and Supplies. Get together the following list of items in preparation for the activity:

- handout (activity 9-1)
- flipchart paper
- colored markers
- masking tape to post flipcharts.

Step-by-Step Design.

1. Before class, put stickers on the direction sheets (activity 9-1) to break people into groups of three to five. For example, if there are going to be 20 people in the session, you get five different kinds of stickers to create five groups of four people. Assume you are using five different colored stars. Put a colored star sticker on each of the handouts and shuffle the handouts so the colors are mixed up. As you pass the sheets out, people who sat together will probably get different color stars.

2. Welcome everyone and pass out the direction sheets.

3. Ask people to read through the directions. See if they have any questions. At this point, they may have already started figuring out at their table who is the project manager. Surprise them by pointing out the star sticker. Instruct them to find the other people on their team and sit with them to do this project.

4. Each team needs flipchart paper and colored markers. Make sure each team has one less marker than the number of people.

5. Begin the project and start timing (15 minutes).

6. When 5 minutes passes, let the teams know that time is up in 10 minutes. Explain that each team must send the member currently drawing to work on another team (clockwise) right now. Manage the chaos of this request!

7. When 5 minutes passes, let the teams know that time is up in 5 minutes. Explain that on each team, the only person who can write on the poster from this point forward is the project manager.

8. After 15 minutes passes, ask everyone to stop. Give them an additional 5 minutes to prepare their presentation strategy.

9. Have the teams present their posters. Enforce the 2-minute rule.

10. Debrief this project.

Tips. As you have probably figured out, although this activity helps people vent, it also simulates a real project with real problems. Moving resources in the middle of the projects is not unusual and neither is a project manager trying to do the whole thing alone. Other challenges simulated by this activity are time constraints, resource skill differences, team challenges, and limited supplies.

Top Priority

Be careful not to point out interesting behaviors until the debrief. Observe the teams, and make notes on language and actions to talk about later. In this case, you are going to debrief this activity around two things: the span of emotions—positive and negative—that are uncovered, and the project issues demonstrated. Make notes on flipchart paper as you summarize the discussion regarding these questions:

- What are some of common issues that have come out of these posters?

- What has hindered the adoption of the methodologies in the past?

- How have methodologies helped people in the past?

- What are some critical steps that must be taken for this methodology to work?

- Let's talk about this "project." What hindered the success of your project? What problems did you encounter?

- What would you do differently if you were to do this project again?

- What did you do extremely well on this project?

- How was this project like the real world?

Results. The team discovers that the fears that they have about the project—lack of control, too much documentation, slower completion—are also creating the challenges in their project behavior. For example, by not doing much planning up front, the projects can spin out of control when under pressure. Projects can't just depend on one super project manager, which can happen when the project is not well understood. At this point, the participants begin to see that they really do need some structure around their projects to be more successful.

Overview

Learning Objectives. After completing this experience, the participant will be able to define the phases of the new methodology and apply the methodology using a flexible structure.

Required Equipment and Supplies. Assemble these items prior to the session:

- the job aid (activity 9-2) laminated or reproduced on card stock
- PowerPoint slide of activity 9-2
- PowerPoint projection equipment (LCD projector, screen).

For more information on this project management model, see Russell (2000).

Step-by-Step Design. Following these steps can help ensure the success of the overview session:

1. Pass out the job aids to the participants.

2. Display the model on the screen using PowerPoint slides.

3. Go through the mnemonic first ("Dare to Properly Manage Resources") and explain how the first letter of the mnemonic indicates the first letter of the phases Define, Plan, Manage, and Review. I often ask people to guess which of these phases is the one the U.S. business world is best at? The answer is manage. We have a culture of "just do it," and tend to skip define, minimize plan, and ignore review altogether, thereby dooming us to repeat the same mistakes.

4. Go through each of the phases, using examples to open the topic when possible.

   - Define—the *why* of the project. It answers the question, "Why is the business funding and doing *this* project rather than something else?" This phase creates a project charter.

   - Plan—the *how* of the project. It answers the question, "Now that we understand why, how are we going to do the activities and assign people to get this project done?" The plan phase creates a project plan.

   - Manage—the *do it* of the project. It answers the question, "Now that the project has started and everything has changed, what do we do?" This phase creates an updated project charter and plan. Flexible structure comes in to play, because there's always a plan, but the team is ready to change it if necessary.

■ Review—the *learn* part of the project. After the project is done, it answers the question, "Now the project is over, what have I learned to help me manage projects better the next time?"

5. Point out the deliverables in each of the phases. Go through each at a high level.

Tips. More than likely, you will have to modify this activity for your own methodology and terms. If you are training on a project management methodology, it is important that you tell participants about the Project Management Institute (www.pmi.org). This is a nonprofit research organization that publishes and maintains a model called the PMBOK (Project Management Body of Knowledge). It is important that all project management methodologies be aligned to it.

Sequence

Learning Objectives. After completing this experience, the participant will be able to list, define, and sequence the deliverables of the project management methodology.

Required Equipment and Supplies. For this game, you need cards for the deliverables of the methodology (activity 9-3) and instruction sheets for each player.

Step-by-Step Design. Here are the steps you should follow for implementing Sequence:

1. Break the participants into new teams of three to five participants.

2. Pass out a deck of the cards to each team.

3. Review the instructions with the group and demonstrate by playing one hand.

4. Round 1: Have the teams play with their cards publicly out in front of them, using the job aid freely.

5. Round 2: Have the teams play with private hands and without the job aid. The job aid may be used to validate the winner.

Tips. This is a very powerful exercise, but it is new to most people. Be thorough when you go through the instructions and demonstrate the play. Keep in mind, too, that 24 steps is many, many steps! To make the game faster, consider playing with 10 cards. They will still have to be in order, but the order won't be all the deliverables. This will make the winning hand different every time but still encourages the understanding of flow of the methodology.

Top Priority

Debrief this activity by asking, "What deliverable was most difficult for you to figure out?" and "What did you figure out that helped you keep the deliverables in order?"

Results. At this point, unbeknownst to them, the participants are very familiar with the language, concept, use, and sequence of the new methodology.

Same/Different

Learning Objectives. After completing this experience, participants will be able to choose activities that will help their own projects as well as the adoption of the methodology.

Required Equipment and Supplies. All you need for this activity are the scribing sheets (activity 9-4).

Step-by-Step Design.

1. Break into new teams of three to five participants and distribute the first brainstorming scribing sheet.

2. Go over the directions with the team, and ask them to complete the first round of brainstorming in 5 minutes. Be clear that points will be awarded to teams with *unique* ideas that no other team thinks of. Say that if teams are not laughing, they are not doing it right.

3. When time is up, ask for a volunteer to take notes on the flipchart. Ask each team to share one idea they think will be unique. Check that no other team has it. If they do not, award that team a point, and log the idea on the flipchart.

4. Repeat the sharing of one unique idea three times (so each team has been able to share three unique ideas).

5. Pass out the second brainstorming scribing sheet.

6. Go over the directions with the team, and ask them again to complete the brainstorming in 5 minutes. Be very clear that this time points will be rewarded for ideas that another team has, different than the first round.

7. When time is up, ask for a new volunteer to scribe at the flipchart. Ask each team to share one idea they think will be unique. Check that another team has it. If they do, award that team a point, and log the idea on the flipchart.

8. Repeat the sharing of one idea three times as before.

9. Give the winning team a prize.

Tips.

■ Keep this activity moving. I physically walk around the room and go to the team when it is their turn to share an idea. If people take too long to answer, it kills the excitement of the mock competition.

■ Only share three ideas. If you try to share all the ideas from each team, it gets really boring.

■ Help teams who are having trouble brainstorming get started by seeding their discussion with crazy ideas, for example, "If we hacked into the

Project Management Institute's Website and destroyed it, no project management methodology could survive."

■ Steer teams away from ideas that get too bizarre, like "We could kill all the project managers." Encourage them to be creative within the limits of possibility.

Top Priority

Ask the class to look at the list of crazy destructive ideas. How can these be flipped around and made into productive ideas? (Gather these ideas on the flipchart.) Now have the class look at the list of productive ideas. Which ideas would work? Ask the participants to identify ideas that they could help with.

Results. The team has done a nice job coming up with productive ideas they can help with. Now, the participants have started to identify themselves as owners of the methodology and its success.

Personal Action Plan

Learning Objectives. After completing this experience, the participant will be able to commit to helping make the new project management methodology successful.

Required Equipment and Supplies. All you need for the action plan is the contract with the project office (activity 9-5).

Step-by-Step Design. Follow these steps:

1. Pass out the contract and explain that this is only a mental exercise and no copies will be kept by anyone but the individual. Ask each person to silently fill out the contract.

2. Ask people to pair up and share their contracts one another.

3. Reconvene the full group and debrief.

Tips. These suggestions can guide you during implementation of the personal action plan.

■ This is the session closer. It is possible that you will have objections from participants here, but the form is designed for them to express the objections through writing.

■ By pairing up, people will help each other work through some of their concerns.

Top Priority

Debrief and close, by asking the following:

■ What are some of the challenges that you are worried about going forward with this new methodology?

■ What are you personally afraid you might lose?

- What do you hope to gain?

- What are some of the ways that you can help make the methodology successful for you and for others?

To conclude, ask all the participants to share one action they will take as they return to their projects.

Results. The participants leave as knowledgeable and empowered advocates of the methodology.

Resources

Learning Objectives. After completing this experience, the participant will know how to research specific questions regarding the project office and the project management methodology.

Required Equipment and Supplies. For this organizational step in the intervention, you need the list of resources (activity 9-6).

Step-by-Step Design. As people leave, give them the resource list to take with them. Alternatively, you could put the resource list online.

Measuring Your Success

For the most meaningful results, the evaluation should be done as if the owners of the rollout completed it, not performance consultants. Help the project office set up one or all of the following:

- a list of projects well under way before the new methodology and the success rates

- a list of projects using the new methodology and the success rates

- occasional interviews with people to document how the rollout is going

- participation in post-project review to log lessons learned so they can be applied with new projects and help the project office to improve project management.

Debrief

Rolling out new procedures, especially new methodologies, is so difficult that it is almost never completely successful. But part of the reason for the lack of success is the measurement of what success really is. Success in this type of initiative can never happen in a day or a week or even a year. When success does occur, that is when people are using the methodology so naturally that they don't even notice, it is usually at least 18 months down the road.

Most methodology rollouts are successful. People learn to add the good ideas to their personal toolbox each time a new method comes through. Sure, most companies have tried so many different methodologies that the teams are a bit cynical about a new one. However, improvement is still usually an outcome, even if it is a few steps forward with one step back.

The big mistakes made when rolling out new processes are to:

- sell it as if you are married to it (You will be beaten to a pulp!)
- sell it as if it were perfect (You will be ignored).

Instead, position the methodology as an evolving way of thinking, as a language for communicating with others as projects get larger, more complex, and more risky and as they cross more parts of a business.

In the next chapter, we'll move from the whole organization to the relationship between a supervisor/coach and his or her subordinate. Coaching is a huge challenge to middle management and one that training is often called on to help with.

Activity 9-1. Venting.

In this project, you will have 15 minutes to create a colorful poster on flipchart paper. You will be provided with flipchart paper and markers. Here are the project requirements:

- Your team will build a poster representing all the rumors you have heard, both negative and positive, about the new project methodology and the project office.
- Your poster must include words and pictures. The more creative, the better.
- Your team can only use the supplies that you have.
- Your team must build the poster in this room.
- Each team member must write or draw at least one thing on the flipchart.
- The project manager will be the person with the most years at the company.
- Each team will present their poster to the rest of the class. You will be given 2 minutes.

Activity 9-1

Activity 9-2. A mnemonic device for learning the basics of project management.

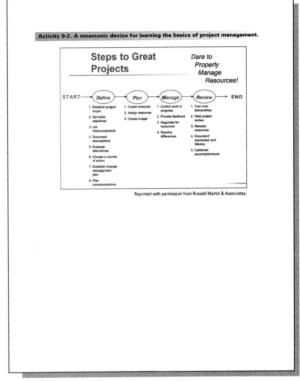

Reprinted with permission from Russell Martin & Associates.

Activity 9-2

Activity 9-3. Sequence card game.

Instructions for play:

The dealer will shuffle the cards. He or she will deal exactly 24 cards to each player. *The players must keep the cards in the order (front to back) that they were dealt to them.* The dealer will put the pile of remaining cards upside down in the center of the table and turn the top card over, starting a discard pile.

TIP: To make play easier and help learning occur, encourage the players to lay all their words out in front of them on the table for all to see.

To take a turn:

A player *must* pick up a word from either the draw pile (upside-down cards) or the player can also take the *last* discard. (Players may not take any cards that are underneath the last card.)

The player may then replace any of his or her cards with the new card. If it isn't useful, the player may discard the new card. To end the turn, the player *must* discard one card by placing it face up on the discard pile.

Play continues until someone has the sequence complete. The job aid can be used as a reference *or* as the check at the end.

1	DEFINE
2	Establish project scope
3	Set initial objectives
4	List risks/constraints
5	Document assumptions
6	Evaluate alternatives
7	Choose a course of action
8	Establish change management plan
9	Plan communications
10	PLAN
11	Create schedule
12	Assign resources
13	Create budget
14	MANAGE
15	Control work in progress
16	Provide feedback
17	Negotiate for resources
18	Resolve differences
19	REVIEW
20	Turn over deliverables
21	Hold project review
22	Release resources
23	Document successes and failures
24	Celebrate accomplishments

Make copies of the words only. (The numbers represent the sequencing order, and are just for the facilitator to check correctness if there is a debate within a team.)

For the sake of table space, do not make these word cards too big.

For every one person on a team, you will need two sets of the words.

For example, a team of four would need eight sets of the words shuffled to play the game.

Activity 9-3

Activity 9-4. Same/Different scribing sheets.

Round 1

In your team, make a list of as many ideas as possible to answer the question:

"How could we screw up the adoption of this new methodology?"

Your team will win if you have the *most unique* suggestions compared to the other teams' ideas. You have 2 minutes. List your ideas below:

Round 2

In your team, make a list of as many ideas as possible to answer the question:

"How can we ensure that the new project management methodology will help projects?"

Your team will win if you have the most suggestions that are *the same* as any other teams. You have 2 minutes. List your ideas below:

Activity 9-4

Activity 9-5. Contract with the project office.

I, _____, agree to work with the project office to improve
project management at this company. I agree to take the following actions immediately to help in this regard:

1. _____

2. _____

3. _____

I will leverage the resources available through the project office to help me with:

1. _____

2. _____

3. _____

Signed _____

Activity 9-5

Activity 9-6. Resources available for project management.

Documentation Available:

Resource	Location
Frequently Asked Questions	Project Office Website
Methodology Detailed User Guide	Project Office
Job Aid	Project Office

Training Available:

Resource	Location
Getting Started With Project Management	Workshop—Training Department
Project Management Basics	e-learning
Project Kickoff	Performance Consulting Department

Outside Resources Available:

Resource	Location
Project Management Institute	www.pmi.org
Project Management for Trainers, a book by Lou Russell	www.astd.org
NASA Ask magazine	www.nasa.gov

Activity 9-6

chapter 10

Coaching

We Hate Coaching!

An executive calls you to ask for help. A recent employee survey indicated that staff were not happy with the coaching they were getting from their managers. There has been a slow but steady decline in the managers' coaching rating over the last 5 years. Turnover has increased slightly, and there is some evidence from exit interviews that this lack of coaching is the problem.

What They Say—The Situation

You: What has happened that triggered this call?

Executive: We do an employee survey every year. Over the last 5 years, the rating for "coaching from your manager" has fallen, and this year it has fallen again. We've also seen an increase in turnover. Some of the complaints voiced during exit interviews indicate that there was little or no career growth opportunity and that the manager did not support their career development. We think this might be tied to coaching as well.

You: So, it sounds like you would like to improve the managers' ability to coach their people more effectively. Are there any other issues that might be contributing to this problem?

Executive: This is an engineering company, so we hire very strong technical talent. Our managers come from the technical side, and being technically oriented, they are often not comfortable with the supervisory role. Honestly, we've never trained them in how to supervise people, we just promote them. These managers get great marks for being able to help their staff with technical problems, but they aren't great at coaching on performance issues where there will be conflict or on helping people plan their career strategy.

You: So, you would like the managers to feel more comfortable in their role as supervisor. You would like them to be able to coach performance issues and career growth planning as easily as they help their staff with technical problems.

Executive: Yes, that's it! If you could teach them some techniques and processes similar to those that they've had in their engineering programs, it would help them feel more comfortable with that supervisor role.

What You Hear

Your conversation with the client and your research has brought you to the conclusions outlined in table 10-1.

Table 10-1. Logical conclusions.

What the Client Says	What You Hear
The managers need training on how to coach more effectively.	Because we have been doing these surveys for many years, I am very confident that our problems are related to the lack of coaching ability of our managers.
Turnover is increasing.	Turnover may be increasing for other reasons, but there is some evidence that people left because their career planning goals were not being met. This problem could directly relate to coaching.
The managers are highly technical.	These managers have been rewarded for their technical abilities. Both in their academic backgrounds and work backgrounds, little or no time has been spent on teaching them to manage people.

You build agreement with the executive that the goals of the manager program are to:

- reduce turnover and increase staff satisfaction by enhancing the managers' ability to coach

- provide a process and techniques for technical managers to use when coaching on performance problems and career growth planning

- providing training for the 25 managers who will be attending this workshop.

What You Do

Begin where all good performance solutions begin—with asking the right questions. Your training and performance instincts have already given you some good guidance, but like all successful interventions, you first have to figure out what's really behind what is said. Here are some questions that need to be asked before the solution can be proposed:

- What are the specific coaching settings that seem to be the biggest problem? How could I validate this?

- How much of the managers' time is designed to be used for coaching staff? What other job responsibilities do they have?

- How is coaching ability rewarded for a manager? Is it in the managers' job descriptions and is it assessed in their performance reviews? What are the competencies measured?

Results of Questions

In this example, from asking questions you've learned the following:

- The largest coaching issues seem to be career planning, developmental feedback, goal setting, and follow-up.

- No one has ever defined what percentage of a manager's job should be dedicated to developing people. The executive has agreed to consider adding this to the job description, but in the interim, the class will teach that a manager should spend 25 percent of his or her time face to face with staff.

- Responsibility for career planning and feedback for staff will be added to the managers' job descriptions and performance reviews in the next iteration.

Your Triage Intervention

Through detailed discussion with the executive, you have identified two project constraints. First, the coaching techniques to be taught in the class will be reviewed with the executive 1 month before the training materials are built. The other constraint is that the manager session will be held in 2 months. Keeping these restrictions in mind, you have proposed to the executive the plan elucidated in figure 10-1, which he has accepted.

- Prerequisite Behavioral Assessment using the DISC activity (see figure 3-2).

- A 1-day workshop on the coaching leveraging the following activities:

  — Coaching Simulation. **Purpose:** Build skills and confidence by utilizing coaching simulation (activities 3-4, 3-5, 3-6, and 3-7 in chapter 3)

Figure 10-1. Your coaching intervention.

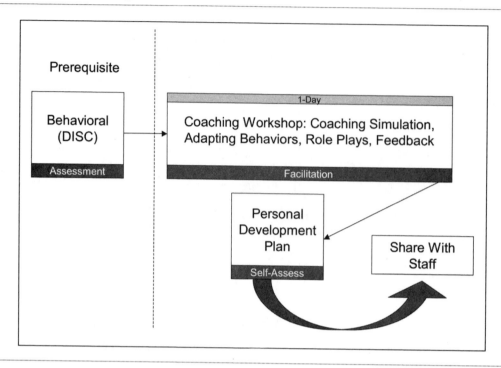

— Behavioral Assessment Review: **Purpose:** Adapt behavior and communication styles amenable to career planning and feedback discussions with staff

— Guardian Angel Role Play. **Purpose:** Practice typical coaching scenarios (activity 10-1; see also activities 3-8 and 3-9 in chapter 3)

— Giving and Receiving Effective Feedback: **Purpose:** Practice typical feedback scenarios

— Personal Development Plan: **Purpose:** Develop a plan for improving abilities related to career planning and feedback (activity 10-2).

The prerequisite DISC assessment will be used to help people understand their own preferences as they begin to coach others to improve. The workshop time will focus on practicing good coaching technique. The powerful component comes from the Personal Development Plan. By sharing this plan with their teams, the coaches will build trust by modeling open behavior. More details about the performance solution are in the following sections.

1. Prerequisite Behavioral Assessment

The prerequisite assessment will be used to provide an accurate perspective to the coaches about their own strengths and weaknesses. You decide to use Quick 'n'

Dirty DISC (figure 3-2) to help each senior consultant understand his or her behavioral strengths quickly. This will help them avoid the assumption, common to coaching, that the people being coached look at things the exact same way the coach does. Part of the workshop will analyze results of this assessment. You hope to fund complete DISC assessments when the coaches buy into the learning.

2. A 1-Day Workshop on Coaching

The workshop will begin with a coaching simulation right at the start. This helps magnify the behaviors that are currently not working during coaching settings.

3. Coaching Simulation

In this simulation, a difficult verbal puzzle will be solved by a person who has a coach. (See activities 3-4, 3-5, 3-6, and 3-7 described in chapter 3.) Two other people will observe the behaviors. What the person being coached doesn't know is that the coach has the puzzle solution. Much learning will occur when the class as a whole discusses why the coach did or did not give out the solution.

4. Review of the Behavioral Assessment

Using the coaching simulation results as examples, the class will go over the behavioral assessment language. There will be plenty of language and decisions observed during the simulation that can be used to point out how different behavioral preferences affect a person's choices.

5. Guardian Angel Role Plays

At this point in the workshop, the participants have learned their own personal challenges in coaching and how to identify them through behavioral assessment. It is time to put their strengths into practice by putting them through a technique called Guardian Angel (activity 10-1 and activities 3-8 and 3-9 from chapter 3). Because role plays are often the most feared classroom activity, each role is assigned two people who help each other. This makes the experience safer and helps the participants adopt new behaviors.

6. Giving and Receiving Effective Feedback

A key component of coaching is giving and receiving effective feedback (activity 10-2). In this section, the students will apply their newly practiced skills for developmental feedback and positive feedback. Participants will also learn skills for receiving constructive feedback.

7. Personal Development Plan

For true behavioral change to occur, participants will create a personal development plan (activity 10-3). They will share their action plan with their staff as they begin routine one-on-one coaching sessions. This will help them keep focused on the changes they want to make and model for their staff what will be expected of them going forward.

What You Build

Quick 'n' Dirty Behavioral Assessment

A DISC behavioral assessment (figure 3-2) was done for each of the participants. This Quick 'n' Dirty assessment begins a person's learning about his or her:

- Preferred behaviors: his or her concern for tasks, people, urgency, and diligence
- Adapted behaviors: how different his or her existing behaviors are from his or her preferred behaviors.

The greater the difference between preferred and adapted behaviors, the greater the stress. When coaching, it is important to identify how a person is trying to be what he or she is not and help that person return to behaviors that are more comfortable for him or her.

One-Day Coaching Session

Learning Objectives. Each future coach will be able to:

- identify his or her coaching strengths and challenges
- explain how to adapt coaching behaviors to others
- ask the person being coached to set goals of a coaching session
- give effective positive and developmental feedback
- create a personal action plan to improve coaching aptitude.

Required Equipment and Supplies. As the trainer, you need to provide the following:

- flipcharts
- markers
- handouts required for each activity.

Chunking Coaching Simulation

In this example, a Thiagi exercise called Chunking is used to catch people in their default coaching behaviors. This is the same exercise that was used in chapter 3 (activities 3-4, 3-5, 3-6, and 3-7). Use phrases that are common in the organization for the Chunking coaching simulation.

The results of this activity show the emerging coaches that they:

- tend to *tell* versus *ask* when in a coaching situation
- feel obligated to help a bit too much, rather than grow the person they are helping
- seldom think to ask the person being coached how much help he or she really wants!

Learning Objectives. Each participant will learn about his or her own coaching strengths and weaknesses by either participating as an observer, a person being coached, or a coach.

Required Equipment and Supplies. Prepare for the activity by assembling the following items:

- flipcharts and markers
- Chunking worksheets (look back to activities 3-4 through 3-6)
- observation worksheet (look back to activity 3-7).

Step-by-Step. By following this sequence, you successfully implement the Coaching Simulation:

1. Break into teams of four to five participants each. Determine the roles each person will play by saying the person with the most children will play the role of the coach. (The number of pets can be the tiebreaker if need be.) The person with the least years of service with the company will play the role of the person being coached, and all remaining people will be observers. Explain that observers will take notes on what they observe, specifically noting any behaviors, phrases/language used, emotions, success/failures, what goes well, what could be improved. *Observers, however, may not help or speak.*

2. Ask each of the coaches to come up to the front for some private instructions from you. At this time you will pass out the hint and solution sheets quickly with very little discussion (activities 3-5 and 3-6). If they ask you if they can tell the person the answer, tell them they can do whatever they want.

3. Pass out the Chunking worksheet (activity 3-4) and explain how to solve the puzzle. Give each team 10 minutes to solve the puzzle.

Tips. Here are a few suggestions to help the simulation run smoothly:

- Use as few instructions as possible; you are trying to catch people in less-than-great coaching behaviors.
- Monitor the room to ensure that observers are observing and not helping. It is really hard to stay out of it.
- If possible, capture some language to share during the debriefing as you wander around. Observe emotions and look for language that expresses that emotion.

Top Priority

Debrief using the following process:

- Ask each person to write down at least one thing that went well and one thing that could be improved in the coaching exercise.
- Ask the observers to share their answers first and place them on flipchart pages.
- Ask the people being coached to share their answers.
- Finally, ask the coaches to share their answers.
- Announce to the group that the coaches had the answers all along. Ask the coaches why they didn't just give the answers to the person being

coached. Ask the people coached how they feel about the fact that the coach did or did not give them the solution. Why did this happen? Stress the importance of a coaching session being driven by the unique needs of the person being coached.

■ Ask each leadership participant to begin their Personal Development Plan (activity 10-3) to begin to clarify his or her strengths, weaknesses, and actions around coaching.

Behavioral Assessment Review

Figure 3-2 is a Quick 'n' Dirty version of DISC to use as a fast and inexpensive alternative to a complete DISC assessment. Only use this version as a last resort; the full version would provide much stronger learning and business return.

Activities 3-1 and 3-2 can be used to interpret DISC results. In this situation with the technical coaches, you find that:

■ Many of the coaches preferred checking off tasks and were not as oriented to growing people.

■ Most coaches were gifted technically but were not "people" people.

■ Some of these senior consultants were not comfortable as coaches and were adapting significantly, causing great stress.

Required Equipment and Supplies. For this activity, all you need are handouts containing figure 3-2 and activities 3-1 and 3-2 for each participant.

Step-by-Step.

1. Distribute the assessments to participants, if possible, in advance of the time together.

2. Encourage the participants to bring the results with them. Be prepared with blank assessments in class in case they forget. Distribute copies of the interpretative activities (activities 10-1 and 10-2).

Tips. These ideas will help achieve success with the behavioral assessments:

■ It is critical that the results remain completely anonymous. Assessment results should never be shared with anyone other than the assessment-taker unless permission is given in advance.

■ The results are generally accurate, but never exact. In this case, the Quick 'n' Dirty assessment will tend to be less accurate than a complete profile.

Encourage each participant to be open to the results even if they do not seem exactly right. I have found that the people who are most bothered by the results have the most to discover and require you to have great patience and gentleness.

Top Priority

Whether debriefing as a group or one on one, follow these steps:

1. Ask each person to reflect on his or her results and to pick one strength and one weakness.

2. If working as a team, break into small groups of three to five participants each to share thoughts.

3. In either a team or in a one-on-one situation, ask each person to share an example of a time when he or she succeeded because of a strength. Ask the team to help brainstorm why the situation went well.

4. In either a team or in a one-on-one situation, ask each person to share an example of a specific time when he or she struggled because of the weakness chosen. Ask the team to help brainstorm other ways the situation could have been handled.

5. Now ask each leader to think of people they have difficulty communicating with. Could it be a behavioral or motivation difference? How could that be addressed?

6. Ask each participant to revisit their Personal Development Plan (activity 10-3) and make notes on how to address behavioral challenges when coaching.

Coaching Role Play: Guardian Angels

At this point, the participants have done coaching role plays and learned about their behavioral strengths and challenges. Through this safe role play, all participants will have an opportunity to practice the behaviors they have just learned and have begun to see success.

This role play is set up to challenge the new coaches. It is designed to encourage misconceptions and poor judgments from both the coach and the coached. Watch for these to occur because that's when learning will occur.

Required Equipment and Supplies. Assemble the following items prior to the role-play activity:

- role-play handout (activity 10-1)
- flipcharts and markers.

Step-by-Step. These are the steps you use to implement the Coaching Role Play:

1. Pass out the scenarios for the role play (activity 10-1). Give everyone a few minutes to read through the scenario.

2. Break into teams of four to five participants each. Ask for one volunteer from each team to coach first. Ask for one other volunteer from each group to be the coach's guardian angel. That person's job will be to help the coach prepare for the coaching session and the coach can freeze the action at any time

during the role play to get help from the guardian angel. (Look back at the Guardian Angel activity in chapter 3 for additional guidance.)

3. Ask for one of the remaining team members to volunteer to be the person being coached.

4. Begin the role play in each team. Let it go on for approximately 10 minutes.

5. Debrief the activity by asking each team to make a list of what went well and what could be improved.

6. Debrief as an entire class, and ask each group to share one learned lesson. Capture these on a flipchart.

7. Change the role of the team members around and have them do another role-play scenario.

8. Debrief the same way.

Tips. Be careful to keep this a positive experience. It will be hard for some people, and stressful, but the guardian angels will be a help. Keep emphasizing the importance of learning from the experience, but remember that changing behavior is very hard because we don't always see our own behavior clearly. Continue to talk about how the participants will notice ways to adapt their own behaviors to the needs of someone else and that each coaching situation is unique.

Time permitting, be prepared to adapt the coaching scenario to a situation similar to one from their real experiences.

Top Priority
Whether debriefing as a group or one-on-one, follow these steps:

■ Ask each person to think about what went well and what could have been improved in the coaching role play. Individually, have each person write down three of each if possible. Have them share these ideas and have one person at the table make a list. Start with the observers and finish with the coach and guardian angel.

■ Bring everyone back together, and ask each team, in turn, to share one thing that went well and one area of improvement that no one else has said yet. Capture these on a flipchart.

■ Repeat for additional role plays.

■ Ask each leadership participant to build upon his or her personal development plan (activity 10-3) to clarify his or her strengths, weaknesses, and actions to close the gaps in the future.

Giving and Receiving Effective Feedback
Required Equipment and Supplies. For this activity, provide the following items:

■ feedback checklist (activity 10-2)

■ Koosh ball.

Step-by-Step.

1. Pass out the handout on giving and receiving effective feedback.

2. Ask people to review the list and discuss any questions they have together in small teams of three to five participants each.

3. Ask with a show of hands: "How many people have more difficulty delivering developmental messages than positive messages?" and "How many people have more difficulty delivering positive messages than developmental messages?" Discuss why this is.

4. Ask everyone to write down two or three responses that he or she might get from a person when delivering the kind of feedback that is most intimidating to them. For example, if someone is uncomfortable with developmental feedback, they might fear a response like "You have no idea the amount of work I do" or "My wife is very ill and I've been under a lot of pressure lately." If someone is most uncomfortable with positive feedback, they might fear a response like "I am just doing my job," or "I'm really not very good at that."

5. Ask everyone to stand. You are now going to lead a "Koosh ball" review of the handout. You will explain that when it is your turn, you will make eye contact with a person, gently toss the Koosh ball to them underhand, and then you will state one of your responses that no one else has shared by saying something such as, "developmental—You have no idea the amount of work I do."

6. The receiver must, as quickly as possible, say what his or her response would be. The team discusses as a whole (for about a minute) how to improve this message. The receiver then repeats the process by tossing the ball to another person and sharing one of his or her responses. After the toss, the receiver sits down so it's clear who has had a turn and who has not.

7. Continue this until everyone has had a turn or, if you have more time, do two rounds.

Top Priority

Debrief by asking the following:

-   What surprised you about the checklist? What was on the checklist that you had never thought about before?

-   What surprised you about the Koosh ball exercise? What made the exercise difficult?

-   Why is it difficult to share both positive and developmental feedback?

After the debrief, ask the participants to return to their personal development plans for the final time. Make sure they have filled out what they are going to do, how it will be measured, and when it will be complete. It is very critical that people not be vague here or the plans will not be useful.

The Personal Development Plan

Building a strong and measurable personal development plan will ensure that change occurs. It is even more important for this session because the coaches will be sharing their plans with the people they coach.

Required Equipment and Supplies. For this activity, all you need is a completed personal development plan.

Step-by-Step. Here are the steps you use to guide the participants:

1. Encourage the participants to take a final look at their personal development plans, ensuring that the actions are measurable, that the measurement is clear, and that all actions have a due date.

2. At this time, ask people to pair up and share their personal action plans with one other person. The purpose is to coach the other person on how to improve his or her personal action plans.

3. As facilitator, you will give each person 10 minutes to get coaching on his or her personal action plan.

4. After the 10 minutes are up, have the person being coached give the other person feedback about his or her coaching. Everyone must share at least one positive observation and one developmental.

5. Have everyone switch to another person, and repeat the process.

Top Priority

Be sensitive to the dynamics of pairing people up, especially in the final personal action plan reflection. It may make sense for you to draw names to pair people up randomly rather than letting people pick.

After the coaching and feedback session, ask participants the following:

- What are the ways they could improve their personal development plans that they discovered through the coaching?

- What feedback was difficult to deliver? Why?

Ask them to revisit their personal development plans and update them with any learning that occurred during the coaching session.

Measuring Your Success

The only way to measure coaching is to ask the people being coached. Encourage each of the coaches to put an action in their personal development plan to get feedback from their staff quarterly.

Debrief

You have reached the end of the specific stories about improving performance through learning. The options are unlimited for innovative, quick, and flexible ways to practice training triage. In the next chapter, you will find some closing thoughts.

Activity 10-1. Scenarios for coaching role plays.

The Situation:

The Olympus Insurance Company sells its automobile and home insurance policies through a network of 3,000 independent insurance agents. These agents are not employees of Olympus, but can act as representatives of Olympus and a number of other insurance companies when they sell policies. The agents are located across the country.

The Issue:

Olympus currently processes new business and handles premium renewals on a mainframe application. They have recently implemented a PC-based system to enter new customers and process renewals. The information will be entered locally by the agent, then uploaded monthly to the home office onto the mainframe's application.

Directions:

You are attending a meeting. In this meeting, you will be trying to uncover what the problem is with the independent insurance agent's client tracking system. Each person will be assigned a role. The goal of this is to try and uncover the actual problem and some possible solutions for further investigation. You will have 10 minutes for the entire meeting.

Role 1:

You are the moderator. You must control the meeting, but you must also find out what the actual problems are and what could solve those problems. You have only 10 minutes to hold this meeting, so things must move quickly. You may use any group technique that you would like.

Role 2:

You are the project manager of the system. This system has only been in production for 1 month, and you don't think there has been enough time for anyone to think anything negative about it. You are very proud of this system, especially since you were able to meet the deadline. You realize that there are certain features that are a little hard to use, but you feel that training (which is not your responsibility) should be able to handle it.

Role 3:

You are a manager in accounting. This month's billing of new clients was the most inaccurate you have ever seen. You have no idea how many clients were billed, but you suspect there are quite a few who were not billed at all. Your service department has been swamped with calls about the inaccurate bills, and you feel that they have reentered almost all the bills that came through on the independent interface.

Role 4:

You are an independent agent who owns a fairly small company and does most of the data entry yourself. You have never used a computer before and have not even installed the software yet, which you are reluctant to tell anybody. The box it came in was so big you are sure that it is going to be difficult to use. You are a fairly quiet person.

Role 5:

You have been a programmer for about 25 years, but you have just recently moved to this department. You know nothing about system development, but you would never admit it. You have been asked to attend this meeting because you may be involved in the rewrite of this system. You like people to think you are smart, so you are constantly bringing up technical issues that are completely off the subject to try and control the meeting and so no one will figure out that you are way out of your league.

Activity 10-1

Activity 10-2. Feedback checklist.

Giving Developmental Feedback

- Base all actions on integrity and genuineness.
- Look for the right time to talk. Keep it as close to incident as possible.
- Use "I" statements.
- Seek first to understand.
- Encourage self-reflection by asking for the person to appraise him- or herself.
- Stick to negative and positive factual content.
- Stick to the issue at hand using specific finite points.
- Clearly articulate what can and should be done.
- Postpone interpretation and avoid inferences or motives.
- Ask for and offer to help.

Receiving Difficult Feedback

- Most people aren't skilled at giving feedback. They will express feelings rather than objective assessment.
- Feedback is perception, not truth. Use feedback for learning about how others perceive you as a starting point for more research.
- Appreciate the time and the courage it took to deliver the feedback.
- Your response dictates the future of feedback to you by this person and perhaps others. Say thank you.
- Learn why the experience was positive or negative so you can leverage the knowledge in the future.
- Balance the span of responsibility and the span of control.
- Entering into this level of dialogue is a significant achievement for you. Congratulate yourself!

Practical How-to's:

- Take notes to keep busy and stay open.
- Let the speaker finish.
- Ask for specific examples.
- Do not defend yourself. Focus on questions.
- Thank the person for his or her honesty.

Giving Positive Feedback

- Base all actions on integrity and genuineness, not manipulation.
- Look for the right time to talk. Keep it as close to incident as possible.
- Use "I" statements.
- Rely on factual content.
- Stick to the issue at hand using specific finite points.
- Postpone interpretation and avoid inferences or motives.

Activity 10-2

Activity 10-3. Personal development plan.

1. *I believe* that my greatest leadership coaching strengths are:

2. *Others believe* that my greatest coaching strengths are:

3. *I believe* that I need to develop the following coaching competencies when working with you:

4. My personal plan for improving our coaching time together is:

-
-
-

(Be sure that the actipns listed in #4 are measurable, that the measurement is clear, and that all actions have a due date.)

Activity 10-3

chapter 11

Final Thoughts
Revealing Solutions

We'd all like to think that training will some day go back to the way it was. We long for the good, old days when we were able to spend months developing a 5-day instructor-led class and then offer it for 2 years through an in-house catalog. Recently, I looked at some of my staff and said, "It appears that complex projects with ever-changing requirements and unclear ownership have become the norm, not the exception." As an industry, it is time that trainers stop waiting for the old days to return. That ship has sailed. Chaos is now the norm.

Nevertheless, these are exciting and interesting times. The important thing is to stay grounded in the need of the customer and the business. If you get distracted by the minute-by-minute preferences of each SME, the fluctuation of the budget, or the irrational need for speed, you will fight your projects as you fight the change. You will not be successful nor will the organizations you serve.

When you stay focused on the customer instead of the change, you can weave and flow with the how-to's of putting a great intervention in place. Notice in this book that training doesn't come in one big package, but in little baby steps with multiple iterations. Get used to not knowing exactly what the whole project will look like. Get used to adapting your solution to what you just discovered in the baby step you just completed.

The wonderful side effect is that the training function will become a valued strategic partner as the organization evolves to meet the needs of the marketplace. We are moving toward the table with the trust of executives in our company who know that we will do more than throw workshops at a problem. Our focus is moving from "what we do" to "what the business needs."

We are the messengers. The solution already exists in the team we are helping. Our job is to help them reveal it and leverage it.

Bibliography

Bridges, W. (2003). *Managing Transitions: Making the Most of Change.* Cambridge, MA: Perseus Books Group.

Goleman, D. (1997). *Emotional Intelligence: Why It Can Matter More Than IQ.* New York: Bantam Books.

Goleman, D. (2000). *Working With Emotional Intelligence.* New York: Bantam Books.

Goleman, D. (2002). *Primal Leadership: Realizing the Power of Emotional Intelligence.* Boston: Harvard Business School Press.

Russell, L. (1999). *The Accelerated Learning Fieldbook.* San Francisco: Jossey-Bass.

Russell, L. (2000). *Project Management for Trainers.* Alexandria, VA: ASTD Press.

Russell, L. (2002). *IT Leadership Alchemy.* Upper River Saddle, NJ: Prentice Hall PTR.

Russell, L. (2003). *Leadership Training.* Alexandria, VA: ASTD Press.

Russell, L. (2005, August 1). "Leadership Development." *Infoline* No. 250508.

Senge, P.M., A. Kleiner, C. Roberts, R. Ross, B. Smith. (1994). *The Fifth Discipline Fieldbook.* New York: Doubleday.

Shackelford, W. (2002). *e-Learning Project Management.* Alexandria, VA: ASTD Press.

Thiagarajan, Sivasailam. (2001). *Performance Intervention Maps: 36 Strategies for Solving Your Organization's Problems.* Alexandria, VA: ASTD Press.

About the Author

Lou Russell

Sitting down to write a bio, one faces the endless question: Who am I? For me, the range of possible answers includes consultant, wife and mother, soccer coach, business owner, church youth leader, community citizen, juggler, fairy tale creator, and solver of impossible problems. I only recently realized that the last role accessorizes all the other hats I wear. The ability to tackle impossible problems is what sets people apart. Successful trainers and business professionals are always part leader, part coach, good communicator, and project manager of everything.

As president and CEO of Russell Martin & Associates, it is my passion to fix impossible business situations. I founded my consulting and training company 17 years ago to bring people together who were committed to helping clients overcome obstacles, maximize profits, improve processes, and operate more successfully. Without exception, achieving improvement always involves project management. The training world may be evolving, but effective learning experiences still need to be fun, flexible, fast, and measurable.

I wrote this book to offer a sampler of reality-based training interventions that you can take with you into the corporate battlefield. Everyone has that moment when he or she doesn't know what to do next and needs an outside idea to get the change process started. I hope you will use this book that I have grown to love to explore some new thinking and experiment with a new training role in the workplace. Try these well-tested strategies for improving the dynamics of your difficult situations.

In case you need to know more about my real qualifications beyond my passion for juggling and fun, I hold an (expired) computer science degree from Purdue University, where I taught database and programming classes, and a master's degree in instructional technology from Indiana University. I am a senior consultant with the Cutter Consortium and serve on the High Tech Task Force in Indiana. Previous books I've written include *The Accelerated Learning Fieldbook* (Jossey-Bass, 1999) and *Project Management for Trainers* (ASTD Press, 1999), *IT Leadership Alchemy* (with Jeff Feldman, Prentice Hall PTR, 2002) and *Leadership Training* (ASTD Press, 2003). You may have read my article contributions in *Computer World, Cutter Executive Reports,* and *Inside Indiana Business,* among others. I also authored *The People Side of Project Management,* part of the Villanova advanced project management certificate program. In 2000, I was honored when Women & Hi Tech named me "Woman of the Year."

You may contact me through my Website (www.russellmartin.com) or via email (info@russellmartin.com).